ALCATRAZ! ALCATRAZ!

CALIFORNIA INDIAN SERIES
BY HEYDAY BOOKS

It Will Live Forever
Traditional Yosemite Indian Acorn Preparation

The Maidu Indian Myths and Stories of Hanc'ibyjim

The Ohlone Way
Indian Life in the San Francisco–Monterey Bay Area

Straight with the Medicine
Narratives of Washoe Followers of the Tipi Way

To the American Indian
Reminiscences of a Yurok Woman

The Way We Live
California Indian Reminiscences, Stories and Songs

ALCATRAZ! ALCATRAZ!
The Indian Occupation of 1969-1971

Adam Fortunate Eagle

FOREWORD BY VINE DELORIA, JR.

PHOTO ESSAYS BY ILKA HARTMANN

HEYDAY BOOKS ☙ **Berkeley**

Produced in cooperation with the
Golden Gate National Park Association

Published by Heyday Books, Box 9145, Berkeley, CA 94709

Cover design by Jeannine Gendar
Interior design by Tracey Broderick
Typeset in Bauer Bodoni
Back cover photograph courtesy of Ilka Hartmann
Cover photograph of Adam Fortunate Eagle courtesy of Beth Bagby

Printed in the United States of America
10 9 8 7 6 5 4 3 2 1

ISBN: 0-930588-51-7
Library of Congress Card Catalog Number: 91-070320

DEDICATION

To the memory of Richard Oakes and his daughter Yvonne, as well as all the veterans of the Alcatraz occupation who are no longer with us. And to American Indians of all tribes who must still be vigilant in protecting their rights and the rights of all their children.

ACKNOWLEDGMENTS

Thanks go to Ron and Nancy Soule for their help, encouragement, and patience in transcribing memories into history.

Wayne Hoff passed through our reservation with an honest, open mind and willingly and skillfully lent a hand at editing.

Charley Money of the Golden Gate National Park Association keeps a belief in truth that serves all who visit and learn from Alcatraz.

William Weyler, author of "Blood of the Land," documented the FBI reprisals against the American Indian Movement.

William Bennett, former Commissioner of the Bureau of Indian Affairs, provided valuable insight on federal actions responding to the occupation of Alcatraz.

Richard Edoes broadened our knowledge of the takeover of Ellis Island.

Jack Forbes and David Risling of D-Q U have a continuing committment to education which serves the cause of all native people.

I thank Bernie Whitebear of Daybreak Star in Fort Lawton, Washington, where the words "Indians of All Tribes" proudly endure and grow in meaning to inspire us all.

Countless unknown and unsung "boat people" risked their property, their reputations, their lives, and even sometimes their pride to serve the cause on Alcatraz.

Tim Findley continues to give support and encouragement.

The news media of the Bay Area kept remarkably open and objective minds to our cause. They could have killed us, but because of their integrity our story still lives.

TABLE OF CONTENTS

ALCATRAZ ISLAND & SAN FRANCISCO BAY

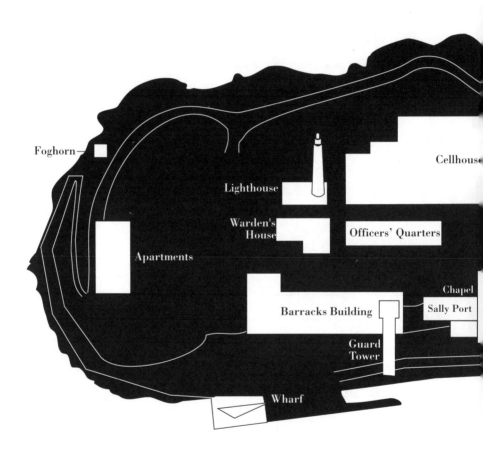

Foghorn

Lighthouse

Cellhouse

Warden's
House

Officers' Quarters

Apartments

Chapel

Barracks Building

Sally Port

Guard
Tower

Wharf

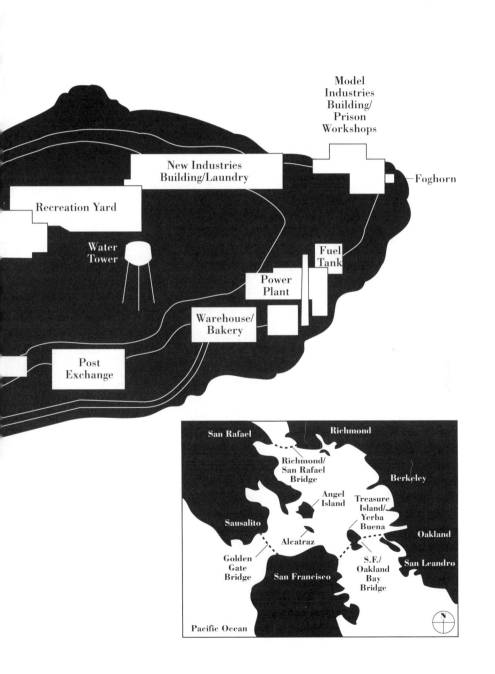

Model
Industries
Building/
Prison
Workshops

New Industries
Building/Laundry

Foghorn

Recreation Yard

Water
Tower

Fuel
Tank

Power
Plant

Warehouse/
Bakery

Post
Exchange

San Rafael

Richmond

Richmond/
San Rafael
Bridge

Berkeley

Angel
Island

Treasure
Island/
Yerba
Buena

Sausalito

Oakland

Alcatraz

Golden
Gate
Bridge

S.F./
Oakland
Bay
Bridge

San Leandro

San Francisco

Pacific Ocean

FOREWORD

Adam Fortunate Eagle, once known as Adam Nordwall, is the trickster incarnate, skipping through swamps and glades where mere mortals fear to tread. It is hard to think of him as an elder—60 years and counting—because in my last encounter with him we looted one of his relatives' fish-smoke houses at Red Lake, Minnesota and had to flee the county before the tribal police incarcerated us. But the fish were delicious and worth it.

Adam was a key player in the Alcatraz occupation and after reading his memories of this prolonged incident which grabbed headlines around the globe, I find that he has omitted all the incriminating incidents that might have gotten him—and a good many others—a permanent residence in Alcatraz or another federal institution. And I lament that he does not thank the Levi-Strauss Company for allowing us to park in their parking lot and escape the harrassment of the San Francisco police when we visited the Indian center in downtown San Francisco. On the other hand, in those days Adam drove a nice new Cadillac and my suspicion is that the Levi-Strauss people figured he was a big stockholder.

Like the later occupation of Wounded Knee, the whole story of Alcatraz is composed of the many memories of people who were involved. Taken together, they present a mosaic of the times—more importantly, our youth and coming of age in a post-industrial society—although we didn't understand it at the time. Alcatraz could not happen today because American society has lost its sense of outrage and its perennial optimism that things can be fixed and made better. We should all mourn the loss of our innocence in that sense.

It does not seem possible, however, that more than two decades have lapsed since the Alcatraz invasion. Rather, Alcatraz seems like another world—a gentler, kinder world at that. My most memorable involvement in Alcatraz—at least the incident with the funniest line— was when I received a call from someone at the Nixon White House telling me to "get those Indians out of that prison or we'll throw them in jail!" But, as the Indians pointed out at the time, Alcatraz with no decent housing, water or employment opportunities was nearer in pro- file to an Indian reservation than were the active federal prisons.

I certainly hope that I am not included in the FBI files in the same way that they characterize Adam. I am, after all, a registered Republi- can and a taxpayer and not a rabble-rousing, Italy-discovering monster like Adam Fortunate Eagle. And this distinction leads me to the final story regarding Alcatraz. Adam was having some trouble—politically— with some of the characters on "the Rock" and was trying to figure out how to handle it. I arrived in San Francisco to discuss possible legislative solutions to getting the island transferred to some Indian organization as an educational center, and Adam met me at the plane and drove me to the docks where the boat for Alcatraz was located.

He insisted on putting his name tag on my sports coat, and when I showed up at the dock some younger Indians read the label and growled: "You'd better not go over there if you know what's good for you." It never occurred to me that these kids believed I was Adam, and since I had taken some controversial stands on other issues I figured maybe these people really didn't like me. We survived the day, and it was not until later, enjoying abalone at Scoma's, that Adam laughed and admit- ted he had set me up to be his stalking horse for the possible confrontation.

I still can't figure out how they could have mistaken me for Adam, because I am considerably taller, much more slender, and very much better looking than he is—and I don't have the swamp-walker limp that is characteristic of Red Lake Chippewas.

Nevertheless, I am pleased to see this book come out—after two decades in the making—and wish Adam the best of everything in be- coming an "arther."

Vine Deloria, Jr.
Boulder, Colorado

TODAY

Life can be a wondrous circle. My wife Bobbie and I were both born on Indian reservations. Bobbie is of the Shoshone tribe and was born on the Fallon Paiute-Shoshone Reservation in Nevada, and I am Chippewa, born on the Red Lake Indian Reservation tucked right up against the Canadian border in northern Minnesota. After a lifetime of adventure we have returned to Bobbie's reservation in Fallon. Now in our sixties, we can enjoy our lives and family, content in the knowledge that our youthful struggles are behind us.

Our lifestyle is a comfortable blend of new ways and old traditional tribal ways. Family gatherings at our home on the reservation center mostly around conventional American holidays, but more traditional tribal gatherings are held as well. As a pipe carrier and ceremonial leader I conduct a variety of ceremonies for both natives and non-natives: wedding ceremonies take place within the sacred circle on our property; a "Wash-Away-the-Tears" ceremony marks the end of a period of mourning for a lost loved one; the Sweat Lodge ceremony cleanses and purifies the participants, who return to the world in a symbolic rebirth. At the conclusion of such ceremonies we share in a bounteous Indian feast with wild game—deer, elk, or buffalo—for the main dish and steaming bowls of Red Lake wild rice, corn on the cob, fry bread, and many other tribal delights as side dishes. Before starting the delicious feast, a plate containing a small portion of each dish and drink is placed on the fire as a way of giving "mi-gwitch," or thanks, to the Great Spirit for the blessings received.

Adam and Milton Ward (Tlingit) at an eagle blessing ceremony. Photo courtesy of Adam Fortunate Eagle.

No one loves these events more than I do. Like a patriarch of old, I sit at the head of the long table loaded down with the sumptuous feast, surrounded by our three children, adopted son, sons- and daughters-in-law, grandchildren, and friends. The presence of three generations makes me feel truly blessed—totally aware of being joyfully involved in the sacred circle of life.

After the feast comes a time of visiting and, on some occasions, storytelling. My granddaughter Mahnee is fascinated with old legends and always begs me, "Grandpa, please tell us a story." So I tell a funny "How" story, like the story of "How the Eider Duck Got Its Red Eyes." When I finish, the children turn to Bobbie. Grandma tells "Water Baby" stories—traditional legends of the Paiute-Shoshone tribes—or tales of "Dogobush," the creature that inhabits the mountains and can harm children if they wander too far from camp during the time of the pine nut harvest. Telling these stories teaches the children of the old ways.

At one of these gatherings, Mahnee asked, "Grandpa, were you ever a warrior?" As I sat thinking about the question, my adopted son, Tim, answered for me, teasing the children but serious as well.

"Yes, your Grandpa was a warrior. A warrior of Alcatraz."

Grandpa was a real Indian warrior! The children all perked up.

"Not a warrior of the old times," I told them, "But a modern Indian warrior."

I then told them the story of the Indian occupation of Alcatraz.

THE 1964 INVASION

More than 20 years have passed since the occupation of Alcatraz, and during that time many misconceptions have been formed about what happened. But the passage of time has also allowed us to mellow out, and it now provides a perspective we did not have when we were in the thick of the action. I look back now at this complex and controversial event and give my version of the story.

Where to begin? I guess the roots of the occupation were first formed when Columbus set foot on an island in the Caribbean. I think if the Indians of that island had made as much fuss as the government of the United States did about the island of Alcatraz, we wouldn't have had the problems that forced us to invade. Maybe we Indians could learn something about holding onto our land and making guests feel unwanted. Yet perhaps we did learn something from what happened after Columbus landed on that island, because in a way, the same also happened out on "the Rock." Nobody really expected us to be that persistent, and certainly no one expected us to stay very long.

The dramatic Indian occupation of Alcatraz, which got so much national and international attention in 1969, actually began five years earlier, in 1964. About a year after the prison closed, a handful of Sioux landed on the island and staked out claims under a 100-year-old treaty permitting non-reservation Indians to claim land the government had once taken for forts and other uses and had later abandoned.

The Sioux "takeover" lasted only four hours, and the next day the *San Francisco Examiner* called it a "wacky" invasion. But the story ran on the front page, and the coverage was pretty straightforward, even sympathetic. All the papers ran stories. The handful of Bay Area Sioux, born on a reservation in South Dakota, had chartered a boat, landed on Alcatraz on the blustery Sunday morning of March 8, 1964, and driven claim stakes into the ground under the Sioux Treaty of 1868. The biggest stories ran in the *Examiner* and the *Oakland Tribune*. They publicized not just the "invasion" but also its underlying goals, which were to test the validity of the 1868 treaty and remind people of the more than 600 treaties which had been broken and other injustices which were still being committed against Native Americans by the federal government. The Indians also wanted to call attention to the ridiculous offer of 47 cents per acre which the government was then proposing to California Indians as compensation for the tribal lands stolen from them since the Gold Rush.

A lot of readers probably did think of the takeover as a comic opera or a stunt. Of course it was a stunt. History is full of stunts that were pulled primarily to publicize a cause. Dumping tea into Boston Harbor was a stunt, and those guys didn't even have the courage to own up to their real identity. They dressed up as Indians instead, but that subterfuge didn't stop the history books from making heroes out of them.

Our men really were Indians, real-life Dakota Sioux, and they wanted the world to know it. The landing party totaled about 40 people, including the five who were going to stake the actual homestead claims, their lawyer Elliot Leighton, a bunch of us from the Bay Area Council of American Indians, and reporters and photographers we had invited to ensure the widest possible publicity for the Indian cause. There was a lot of street theater in the Bay Area in those days, and this was another kind, one which was intended to put its message on a bigger stage via the media. The Sioux principals included Garfield Spotted Elk, Walter Means, Richard McKenzie, Mark Martinez, and Allen Cottier. McKenzie and Martinez were both welders by trade. Allen Cottier, a house painter also known by his Sioux name of Whistler, was president of the Bay Area Council of American Indians, and he acted as leader and spokesperson of the group. None of them could be called a young "hothead." Garfield Spotted Elk, the youngest, was in his late 20s; Mark Martinez was in his early 30s; Dick McKenzie and Walter Means were both in their late 40s; and spokesman Allen Cottier was 42 or 43.

Things got off to a pretty amiable start. When we stepped off our rented boat onto the island, a pickup truck came roaring up to the dock. The fellow at the wheel identified himself as A.L. Aylsworth and said he was the federal caretaker. Elliot Leighton opened his briefcase and politely began to explain the legal issues involved in the landing. He told

Mr. Aylsworth that the Sioux were staking their claims to the island's 20 or so acres of government land that were not being used for specific purposes or had been abandoned.

Aylsworth didn't seem particularly perturbed—after all, the last convicts had been taken off the island a year before and nothing had happened on Alcatraz since that time.

"Well," he told Elliot, "I guess if you want it, you can have it."

This was sort of a surprise, but in keeping with the good-humored tone of the whole undertaking. In fact, throughout the homestead claim the Indians were never anything but dignified and amiable, in contrast to some of the government people who arrived later. One newspaper article eventually described them, with some understatement, as "dour-faced."

Then, with an American flag in the lead and the rest of us following behind, the Sioux homesteaders started exploring the land they had claimed. When they came to a grassy area in between a few drab apartment buildings, they halted. As leader and spokesman, Allen Cottier read a statement. He was wearing his war bonnet, and with the eagle feathers blowing in the wind he looked quite magnificent, as befit a descendant of the famous warrior-chief Crazy Horse. Allen stated that the action was entirely peaceful and in accordance with Sioux treaty rights, and he proclaimed Alcatraz to be surplus land under the Treaty of 1868. He said the Sioux were offering just compensation for Alcatraz— the same 47 cents per acre the federal government had just offered the California Indian tribes for lands illegally taken from them since the Gold Rush. That amounted to about $9.40 for the full rocky island, or $6.54 for the twelve usable acres on the island's flat top. Allen also stated that the Indians would be magnanimous: the government could keep the Coast Guard lighthouse on the island as long as it didn't interfere with the Indian settlement.

Actually, the provision permitting Indians to stake claims on unused government land had been revoked by Congress in 1934, but because of the 1868 treaty a specific exception was made for the Sioux, who had been forced to cede much of their land for the construction of a string of forts. So it all sounded perfectly reasonable.

When Allen finished, everyone cheered lustily and then went to search out the best sites for their homesteads. Garfield Spotted Elk selected a claim with a beautiful view of the mainland and the city of San Francisco, located in a nicely landscaped spot in the center of a flower bed planted with big magueys, flowering cactus, and geraniums. Walter Means' son Russell had come along for support, and he helped his dad pound in his claim stake. Russell, later involved in the uprising at

Wounded Knee, was then about 26. He took one look at the main cell block and then declared, "That miserable eyesore, we have to tear that down."

The claims were written in ink on pieces of deer hide and attached to homemade claim stakes, one of which, as I remember, was made from an old mop handle. After the claims had been properly marked, Leighton had the Indians sign official claim forms to be mailed the next day from San Francisco to the Bureau of Land Management in Sacramento. Tom Brown of the United Council stood atop the stone wall with a large mirror in his hands and flashed the message to the mainland that the mission was accomplished.

The legal formalities were followed by a nice, slow, traditional victory dance performed in the shadow of the Coast Guard lighthouse to the sound of two beating drums. The homesteaders then set up a tent for shelter through what promised to be a cool and windy night.

It was at this point, about two hours into the occupation, that the acting warden, Richard J. Willard, burst onto the scene. Summoned from his home on the mainland, Willard had come across the bay on the prison boat, and it was clear that he saw nothing funny or benign in the situation. A grim-visaged fellow in a derby hat, he didn't want to hear any arguments about rights and wrongs and began shouting that we were all trespassing and violating the law. He was so angry he even shoved a newspaper photographer who had come too close. He and his people were as pickle-faced and infuriated as the Indian homesteaders were amiable. The Indians were clearly unarmed, but perhaps the very idea of Indians frightened the government men. They absolutely lacked any sense of humor, or even a sense of proportion.

Willard repeated that we were trespassing on government property and threatened not just the Indians, but also the reporters and photographers, with dire consequences if we didn't all get off the island immediately. And he warned that if any one of the six-man caretaker garrison got so much as scratched as a result of the trespass, the Indians could be charged with a felony.

At that threat the newsmen and the support group retreated. But the Sioux homesteaders held their ground, at least for the moment. They sat themselves down cross-legged in front of their tent,and waited to see what would happen next. When it became clear after a couple of hours that the next stage could be nasty, Elliot advised them to leave the island since they had made their point and didn't want their action to be confused in the public eye with police-baiting.

So they did. They packed up their camping gear and beat a prudent and dignified retreat just before federal reinforcements arrived in the form of an assistant U.S. attorney and two U.S. marshals, who passed the Indians heading back to the mainland.

Of course, the 1964 action was never meant to be an occupation, and it wasn't. Exactly four hours after the landing the U.S. Government forced the Sioux to leave under threat of arrest and prosecution. But important things managed to get said, and the reporters listened. As a result of the media's interest, the protests of Indian people in the Bay Area got much more public attention than they could have garnered with yet another protest meeting.

The event was publicized and remembered, and it also made some of us wonder whether that gloomy and crumbling fortress might one day be turned into a resource for Indian people. After the brief Sioux invasion, we kept thinking about Alcatraz, and the ball began rolling in the direction of the much bigger and longer-lasting Indian occupation of 1969. What those Sioux really did was begin a dream.

I have to admit, all that media coverage was heavy stuff, but there was also a negative aspect that affected events of the next occupation. We were so impressed by the way our demands and hopes were publicized in the papers that we confused appearance with substance. Some of us thought that if the public was informed about our needs, then maybe there would be pressure on the government bureaucracy to do something about Indian problems. We overestimated the power of the media to affect policy and bring about positive change, especially if that change costs a lot of money.

Yet after 1964 the idea of an Indian Alcatraz was never far from our thoughts, and for a lot of younger Indians it began to assume the aura of almost a Holy Grail. I remember one group of Indian students from San Francisco State going down to Aquatic Park just a few months before the 1969 occupation and standing there on the beach, staring in silence out at the island for more than an hour. It was as if they were trying to use sheer willpower and fervent hope to do what the Sioux pioneers had attempted in 1964—convert a fearsome prison into an Indian Camelot.

We felt that if Alcatraz became Indian country it would, almost by magic, solve all sorts of problems of being Indian in the Bay Area and serve as a beacon of hope and pride for Indian people all over the country. Of course, there were skeptics who tried to point out the pitfalls: the power of government and commercial interests, the problems of communication with the mainland, the lack of fresh water, the deteriorated state of the buildings, and the difficulty of making those grim cell blocks into anything like a livable environment. But nobody wanted to think about that. Alcatraz was a dream, a dream that just had to become a reality.

URBAN INDIANS

I remember that as we were heading back to the mainland that March day in 1964, one of the non-Indians asked another non-Indian, "What are a bunch of Sioux Indians doing here in the Bay Area? Why aren't they back in the Midwest, or wherever they're from?"

I am sure he wasn't the only one wondering why we Indians would be so concerned about a little rock in the middle of San Francisco Bay when we supposedly had vast reservations to live on and the government was reportedly paying us to do nothing. Why would we leave such a paradise and move to the big city where we might even have to work?

If you visit a reservation today you will probably see poverty, alcoholism, and desperation. These problems persist despite improvement due to recent Indian activism, such as the Alcatraz occupation. In 1964, the reservations were much worse. Corruption in the Bureau of Indian Affairs (BIA) and the tribal governments often allowed greedy speculators to purchase tribal resources such as land and mineral deposits; Indians remained poor and their reservations remained undeveloped.

In 1968, a Senate subcommittee stated that "50,000 Indian families live in unsanitary, dilapidated dwellings, many in huts, shanties, even abandoned automobiles." The report went on to state that the average annual Indian income was $1500, 25% of the national average; the unemployment rate among Indians was 40%, more than ten times the national average; the average age of death for American Indians was 44 years and for all other Americans 65 years; infant mortality was twice the national average; and thousands of Indians had migrated or been relocated into cities only to find themselves untrained for jobs and un-prepared for urban life. Many returned to their reservations more disil-lusioned and defeated than when they left. And this report appeared after several years of "Great Society" programs, none of which seemed to be directed towards helping the Indians. For many, reservation life was one of hopeless poverty and ongoing misery.

Many people think that these conditions were due to laziness, a sort of welfare mentality. They don't realize the conditions were a deliberate creation of the U.S. Government, the result of decades of manipulation, contempt, and control.

The government and the speculators knew that the tribes held vast amounts of natural resources. In 1952 the government prepared an 1800-page report on Indian conditions. Indians called it the "Doomsday Book." The report discussed the complicated task of eliminating the reservation system and concluded that the expense and difficulty were justified by the prospect of gaining control of the natural resources held by the tribes. In addition to timber and water, it was estimated that the 23 Western tribes controlled 33 percent of the country's low-sulfur coal, 80 percent of the nation's uranium reserves, and between 3 and 10 percent of the gas and petroleum reserves. I have never seen the monetary value of these tribal holdings quoted in any report, but the amount would have to be very large.

Considering all these natural resources, one would think that the BIA would have trained Indians to develop these resources to create jobs and wealth for all the Indians on the reservation. Self-sufficiency would have been the humane solution, but it might have interfered with the profit that stood to be made. The report stated that by withdrawing federal services to the tribes and eliminating the reservation system the government would save millions of dollars every year. Without any In-dian lands to administer, the BIA, the oldest bureau in the federal gov-ernment, could be shut down. This rearrangement would allow the large corporate structure which operated in concert with the federal govern-ment to quickly grab up the natural resources. The last vestige of Indian country would disappear into the history books, which could then proudly proclaim that "the American Indian has finally become fully assimilated into the mainstream of American society." It all sounded like a twist on the "final solution" idea proposed by another government just a few years earlier.

The next year the government put these plans into action and passed what is referred to as the Termination Act, which allowed them to begin removing the tribes' status as political entities. The process of disman-tling 200 years of a relationship between the U.S. Government and the

American Indians lurched into motion like a giant steam roller. But when the government began to look at closing down the reservations, they ran into an interesting problem: the Indian reservations were full of Indians!

The political leaders in Washington then put their collective heads together and dreamed up another scheme—they would reduce the reservation populations by relocating Indians to urban areas. Of course, this would all be done under the guise of helping the Indians. So by 1958 the decision had been made to establish eight relocation centers in major U.S. cities. Four of those centers were set up in California cities: Los Angeles, San Francisco, San Jose, and Oakland.

The BIA had the responsibility of running an employment assistance program for relocated Indians. Unfortunately, the program was really a carrot on a stick to entice the Indians on the reservations, where many lived in great poverty. The BIA sent agents to the reservations to talk to the unemployed young men and women and even the older unemployed family men. The agents offered to help the Indians find work in a "meaningful job." The hitch was that the jobs weren't on or near the reservations as the Indians hoped, but often more than a thousand miles away from their homes and families.

The Indians that signed up for the program were given bus tickets to whichever center they had chosen. For instance, say a young Indian man chose the Oakland center. When he and his family arrived they immediately reported to the relocation office, which found them an apartment, usually in a ghetto. Every morning the young man checked into the relocation office where he was instructed to sit down and wait until called. He sat in a waiting room with a small television set and a bunch of old magazines while an "employment assistance officer" tried to line up a job interview. He was told that if he didn't report to the office each day his subsistence allowance would be cut off. In the meantime, his wife and kids locked themselves in their apartment, because they were afraid to go out by themselves into the crime-ridden streets. When the BIA found a job for their Indian "client," he was cut off from BIA services after his first paycheck. Many of the jobs were temporary. It didn't take long for the Indian to realize he had been trapped.

After the BIA "cut the cord" with the relocated Indians, those who had been given only temporary jobs had to turn to city, county, and state agencies. But the agencies seldom wanted anything to do with the Indians. They were considered the responsibility of the federal government, not local agencies. It was a terrible dilemma to be told, "You're an Indian, you go to the federal government for help." Or, as one Indian declared, "It's damn tough to go around to these different agencies looking for help and they pretend you don't exist."

In a hearing for the Committee on Urban Indians, sponsored by the National Council of Indian Opportunity in the late spring of 1969, an attorney testified to this problem by stating, "Discrimination is implicit in most of the programs for urban areas." Needy urban Indians found themselves in a new type of entrapment—too poor to go back to the reservation and too "Indian" to receive the benefits of society.

For some, the transition was simply too much to take. The government provided the bus ticket from the reservation to the city, but many Indians hitch-hiked back, more bitter than ever about what they felt was another government trick.

For others who stayed, the adjustment from reservation life to an urban existence proved to be chaotic at best. The pressures of adapting and the frustration of dealing with the agencies was too much for many young Indians trapped in the cities. In one eighteen-month period, there were four suicides reported among Indians in the Bay Area. One year in San Francisco, my own sister was counted among the despairing numbers who could not cope with the urban trap. She slipped a plastic bag over her head and filled it full of a greaseless cooking spray.

By 1958, Bobbie and I and our three children were well off compared to most Indians, but only a childhood memory away from those lost and abandoned feelings that tortured so many others. My education had been limited to BIA boarding schools. First I was sent to the drab, culture-killing school dormitories at Pipestone, Minnesota; later I moved on to what seemed to me the vast and glorious campus of Haskell Indian Institute in Lawrence, Kansas, where I first met Bobbie.

In Pipestone I taught myself to carve the only toys I had out of sticks and scrap wood. In the vocational high school curriculum at Haskell, where I demonstrated an utter lack of aptitude for my father's trade of mechanics, Indian art instructors recognized my doodling talents and led me into commercial art classes. I was considered an "old head" at Haskell by the time Bobbie arrived to study secretarial arts and immediately captured my eye. I remember being astonished, and a little befuddled, when she told me her father raised turkeys, not horses or cattle, in Nevada.

We were married in 1948, and for the first six months of our marriage we were separated while Bobbie worked as a secretary for Stewart Indian School in Nevada and I finished graduate studies in commercial art at Haskell. That winter I got my first job drawing magazine advertisements and layouts for a firm in Kansas City and we were reunited.

Were it not for the Korean War, we might never have left. All four of my brothers were called to serve in that conflict. My mother, Rose, was living in San Francisco at the time and we both expected that I, the last of her sons, would be called next. Bobbie was pregnant with our first child, Cheri, and my mother wanted me and my new family to spend what time was left near her. She found me what I thought would be a temporary job with a termite exterminating company near her home in San Francisco.

It was 1951 when Bobbie and I moved to San Francisco with $300 in savings and all of our possessions in three suitcases. We rented a tiny apartment and began setting up housekeeping on the $48 per week that I earned after taxes.

I endured the mindless racism of being called "chief" and "blanket-assed Indian" on the job, and as it turned out, I was never called for military service. But a year later, at the age of 21, I had passed the state test to become a licensed inspector and a decade later had become a vice president and general manager for a major East Bay termite exterminating firm.

Those early years in the Bay Area were a period of financial struggle and hard work, but I was on my way to becoming financially successful. In fact, by the late 1960s I owned my own business, the First American Termite Company; employed fifteen people; lived in a comfortable suburban home with Bobbie and our three kids; and even drove a Cadillac. Nothing would have been easier than assimilating my roots into middle-class America.

Assimilation was not only tempting, but also encouraged in a society that preferred its Indians to be caricatures. There was no easy path "back to the blanket," as it was termed, but for my young family there was reason—and need—to explore my heritage, and theirs.

We took trips to the reservation at Red Lake or to Bobbie's family home on the reservation in Nevada, but these trips were touring excursions among relics of something that was no longer a real and daily part of our lives. Perhaps we would have lost even that much of our past on the reservation had the times not brought it back to us.

During the Korean War of 1950–1953, San Francisco served as a homecoming hub for returning veterans, many of them Indians we had known from home or Haskell Institute. We would see them passing through on their way back to a culture and a way of life that was still trivialized by an urban American society that wanted to treat Indians as souvenirs. In 1958, we began to notice a surge of young reservation Indians brought to the Bay Area under the federal program of relocation.

Indians began to find each other, partially out of a sense of loneliness and confusion in their new urban surroundings and partially out of an urge to share a cultural identity. First came the picnics in Golden Gate Park that grew into drumming and singing sessions. These grew into a pow wow circuit of social gatherings which, often unconsciously, made their own subtle political statement of cultural unity and affirmation.

So great was the hunger for pow wows that we would gather even when it meant serving a white man's need for a Hollywood version of Native America; such was the case of the Indian Days pow wow at San Jose's Frontier Village amusement park. It was at that pow wow that I first met Cy Williams and my life began to change dramatically. The pow wow was open to all Indians, and even if it served to entertain tourists and sight-seers it also filled our growing need for cultural expression. I outfitted my small son Addie with the head of a fox-fur stole I'd found at a Goodwill store and suited myself in a turkey-feather approximation of something Chippewa, complete with little Christmas bells about one-third the size of those worn by traditional dancers.

When a mutual friend pointed me out to Cy as someone from his own tribe, I was doing my best in what I imagined then to be good traditional style. I realize now my dancing was only a "tinkle, tinkle, tinkle" Hollywood imitation in Cy's eyes. We would, nevertheless, become close lifelong friends and together step out on a new road for urbanized Indians.

Cy and Aggie Williams were Chippewas from the Cass Lake Reservation in Minnesota, located just 50 miles southeast of my own reservation at Red Lake. Without intending to do so, Cy had become something of a success story for the relocation program. With BIA help, Cy worked as a machinist and continued to develop his skills. On the job, he also developed a wiry blue collar grit, a rough-talking independence that always seemed to contrast with Aggie's frail, quiet humor. He and Aggie lived in a pin-neat cottage filled with Indian trinkets, curios, and knicknacks.

Cy's old blue panel van was decorated the same way. Little buckskin dolls sat on the dashboard and decals of animals or Indian faces covered the back end. In later years, many other Indians like Cy would proudly display bumper stickers proclaiming, "I'm Chippewa and Proud of It," or "Custer Died for Your Sins," but in those early years of the 1960s Cy and Aggie were making a statement about themselves with all that was available—touristy trinkets. They were a link back home and a way for Cy to express what he felt like shouting.

"Ah, the hell with it," he'd say in frequent frustration, throwing his arms across his chest as if he were tossing off a cur dog. The four of us spoke often about the problems faced by relocated Indians, and gradually Cy began to pass on to me some of his great knowledge of traditional dancing and our own culture. With Cy and Aggie's help and advice, bit by bit I began to replace my fox-fur and Christmas-bell imitations with the vibrant beadwork and stiff quills authentic and meaningful to our people.

Our neighbors in San Leandro would peer over the fence at us on evenings when Cy rehearsed me and six-year-old Addie in the finer points of traditional dancing. We worked hard as the heavy sleigh bells tied to our ankles chimed to the rhythm of tape-recorded drums and singing.

Picnics that grew into pow wows were being held all over the Bay Area almost every weekend. The government had almost certainly not intended or wanted such a resurgence of traditional gatherings. The relocation program had purposely scattered all its "clients," who were usually offered housing in the same run-down neighborhoods and slums but never too near each other. The pow wows in rented halls and public parks gradually grew under the sponsorship of new Indian clubs. Some of them, such as the Sioux Club or the Navajo Club, formed around tribal identities; others, such as the Four Winds Club, focused on social objectives. Weekend pow wows brought us all together—new drumming and singing groups were formed, news of home was exchanged. All of it, I'm sure, caused the BIA great consternation.

Cy showed great patience with me and Addie as we learned his smooth, flowing approach to traditional dancing. But he had little tolerance for the sufferings and injustices he saw among the increasing numbers of young people and families brought from the reservations. By 1961, Cy had become actively involved in a number of Indian activities, and he served on the board of directors of the newly established Intertribal Friendship House in Oakland, a project of the American Friends Service Committee.

"These guys serving on the board," Cy told me with concern, "are mostly white people. A bunch of good-hearted Quakers who just don't know much about Indians. Shouldn't we be more involved in running our own activities? We have had white people telling us what to do and how to do it for too long now. They should be helping us run Indian programs, not directing us!"

I saw what happened to the Indians in the Bay Area and compared it to "self determination" for the Indian people. I realized that Cy made good sense. "What do you want me to do?" I asked.

"Get involved. Help us. We need Indian leadership. You know how to get things done and that's what we need right now," said Cy, who had begun urging other Indians to get involved in the community. "There are a lot of Indian clubs forming right now, and maybe by working together we could do more good for our people."

We contacted all of the Indian groups that we could find in the East Bay, and after several meetings at the Intertribal Friendship House we decided to form an umbrella organization called the "United Bay Area Council of American Indian Affairs, Inc." This was shortened to "United Council." The Pomo Club, Navajo Club, Haida-Tlingit Club, Chippewa Club, Ladies Club, United Paiutes, Four Winds Club, Intertribal Dancers, Haskell Alumni, Radio-Electronics Training School (R.E.T.S.), Sports Committee, Intertribal Friendship House, and the American Indian Culture Group (San Quentin) were all affiliated with the new group.

The United Council was an Indian mini-version of the United Nations. Each affiliated group had its own representative to the Council, and small name plates placed in front of delegates during the meetings indicated the groups they represented. Millie Barichello of the Creek tribe, representing the Haskell Alumni, was elected secretary-treasurer; Al Hicks, an elementary school teacher representing the Navajo Club, was elected vice-chairman; and I was elected chairman.

It was February of 1962, and this joint organization of diverse tribal and intertribal groups in an urban setting was the first of its kind. Anthropologists and other scholars often use the term "Pan-Indian" to refer to this movement toward intertribal organization, but Indians prefer to use the term "intertribal" instead.

The affiliated groups of the Bay Area were bound together by shared interests and shared concerns for the welfare of our people. Working together, we were able to help maintain a stable Indian community within the larger urban context. Each affiliated group maintained its own identity and conducted its own programs while at the same time exercising its voice in formulating larger community objectives. Their collective voices gave the United Council its strength and direction.The wide variety of activities undertaken by the United Council would have seemed unrealistic to many experts in community affairs. Yet the diverse make-up of the Council allowed us to undertake a wide-ranging set of projects.

Most of our projects tried to help the newly arrived relocatees overcome culture shock as they adapted to their new surroundings. The Intertribal Friendship House provided a setting for Thanksgiving dinners, Christmas parties, and a variety of ceremonial events, and most of the affiliated clubs held their meetings and social activities there. It served as the hub of the Indian activities in the East Bay, just as the Indian Center in San Francisco served the needs of that community.

The Bay Area Indian community continued to grow as Indians kept pouring into the area, and the United Council gradually took on a more "activist" orientation until finally in 1969 it became the driving force behind the occupation of Alcatraz.

BAY AREA URBAN INDIAN COMMUNITY

Herb Simmons, a young California Indian, on a street in Oakland.

A family on Valencia Street in San Francisco.

Indian car in Oakland.

Above: Palo Alto Pow Wow.

Eva Brown, (Sioux), and a friend, at left.

Above: Kenny Jose Maria (Papago) at Intertribal Friendship House.

Dinner at Intertribal Friendship House.

Above: Sarah Brown (Pomo) with her niece Tina Fourkiller and nephew Anthony Fourkiller at the Intertribal Friendship House on East 14th Street in Oakland.

Above: Native American Women's Conference in San Francisco.

Pacific Automotive Center, an Indian-run auto mechanics school in Oakland.

Above: Couple at Oakland Museum Pow Wow.

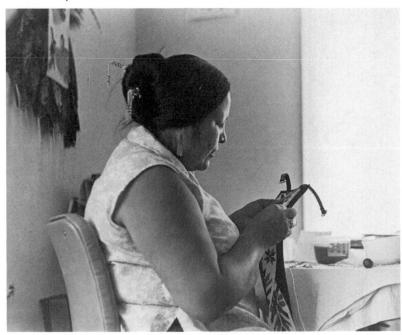

Pauline Campbell (Sac and Fox) doing beadwork at her home.

Dancer at Palo Alto Pow Wow.

PLANS

The United Council met every other Wednesday night at the Friendship House. We sat at folding banquet-room tables arranged in a square that allowed equal space for each of the twenty or so delegates from affiliated clubs. "Indian time" or the demands of a family and a day's work sometimes kept us from starting at 7:30 p.m., but our professional careers and obligations gave our meetings a decorum worthy of any board room. Folding partitions that separated the dining room from the recreation hall could be opened to give us more space, which we ultimately needed as our organized meetings became more like community gatherings of all interested Indians in the area.

I remember the tall, narrow frame of Horace Spencer, a Navajo, standing up to speak of how he, his wife, and their eight children felt marooned and abandoned by relocation. I remember the chuckling good humor shown by Pomos Jim and Alvina Brown, even when they spoke about the bitter struggle of their people to survive official government termination of their tribe in Clear Lake, California.

In some ways, the council meetings functioned like network news programs. They gathered information, shared it among the people, and allowed us to see what was going on in society, specifically the steady attempt to erase the red man's culture from America.

Our council sought no federal grants or government assistance that might further compromise our people. What money we had came primarily from our annual Memorial Day picnic and pow wow. This event usually raised $1500–$2000, which we put into a scholarship fund for children of needy Indian families swept into the confusion of the cities by relocation.

I remember arranging our first Memorial Day pow wow and camp-out. When I was asked to use my business experience in arranging the event, I felt quite proud. The pow wow was to take place at the Bret Harte school in Hayward, which had a beautiful amphitheater with bleacher seating that perfectly fitted all our needs. But we also needed a campground.

I began to campaign for temporary camping space, and the incredulous school superintendent at last accepted my argument that camping out was an essential part of our tradition of remaining in contact with our earth mother. If that was the case, he said, we could use the lawn in front of the school.

I was delighted with the small village of tepees and tents that sprang up that Friday evening. Away from cooped-up apartments, children romped in the grass and parents set about the happy work of preparing for the ceremonies.

My attention was drawn to Jones Benally, a tall, slender Navajo hoop dancer who seemed especially rapt in a ceremony of his own.

"Making medicine," he said simply, "Woman medicine," and flashed me a quick grin.

The pow wow went just as we had hoped: the performance was brightened by many singers and dancers and the bleachers were filled with well-satisfied, paying customers. When it was all over near midnight, I felt elated and proud as I made my way to our front lawn village. Passing the shrubbery, I caught sight of a couple in a private embrace and discreetly looked away.

"I told you so," Benally whispered to me.

It was such a perfect evening. Even Benally's medicine truly worked—the amorous couple later formed a successful marriage. I couldn't believe it all ended with the rainstorm that created bedlam in the quiet camp about 2 a.m.

"Hey!" someone shouted, "It's raining inside my tent!"

Half-dressed and sleepy families of confused children, embarrassed couples, and angry men and women poured out from their tents. Everyone was drenched, and carried their clothes and possessions as if running from a flood.

"It's raining from the ground up!" someone else yelled.

Nobody held it against me for long, but I do still wish the school superintendent had warned me about the automatic sprinkler system.

Despite the humorous difficulties, such events reinforced our unity, which did not come all that easily. White people of this century, even those who think of themselves as liberal and somehow romantically attached to the Indian cause, seldom understand that being "Indian" is something forced upon people of cultures as different as Chinese and Italian. Totally different languages and customs, old rivalries, and even hatreds still stand between many tribes. The unity among them has sometimes been formed out of desperation, mutual agony, or pride.

These differences were laid aside while we met together on the common ground of oppression. We spoke in the mutually-understood language of the white man, with Robert's Rules to guide us out of disputes. There was a pace to our discussions—a rhythm—that kept a careful respect for the anger and sense of loss that we knew many held back.

In 1968, when Alcatraz was declared surplus property to be given to the city of San Francisco, many of us remembered the 1964 Sioux action laying claim to "the Rock." The government had supposedly put that matter to rest in 1965 by concluding that the 1868 treaty with the Sioux applied only to federal lands taken from that tribe and then abandoned. The government said that Alcatraz had never belonged to the Sioux. If it had ever belonged to any Indians, it would have been California Indians, most of whom did not legally exist as tribes in the eyes of the U.S. Government.

Yet the Sioux action conceived by Richard McKenzie had been successful in what it set out to do—point out the government violations of the 1868 treaty and make symbols of them. The useless prison island now symbolized the joking contempt with which the government regarded any native claims.

There it was, a dramatic outcropping right out in the middle of the bay. Every time you crossed the Golden Gate Bridge or the Bay Bridge you saw that little spot in the water and remembered. Even at night the revolving searchlight on the Coast Guard lighthouse beckoned to you. And you thought: "Those twenty acres and all those buildings, all empty, falling apart from neglect. And we have nothing."

Even so, when Alcatraz came up in Council discussions the talk was still only tentative. We had a lot of other projects that occupied our time, our limited resources, and the talents of our people. Alcatraz and the future we envisioned for it only slowly came into focus.

Basically, our initial idea was to write a proposal for the use of Alcatraz by Indian people and then file the necessary application. If this would not work under the terms of the Sioux treaty, then we would try some other arrangement. We were not thinking of taking radical action; another surprise invasion and occupation was then still far from our minds. We were thinking of negotiating with the federal authorities to attempt to acquire Alcatraz peacefully. We didn't even necessarily want the whole island; some portion of it would have been sufficient for a start. Essentially, the message would be this: there is an abandoned prison out there, sitting idle and falling apart. We have a need for it. Let us have it; let us use it.

Of course, we realized that some of the old prison buildings were clearly unsuitable for our purposes. But Alcatraz was a powerful symbol, and we thought it had enough facilities to give it some real potential. Hopefully, we could use that potential to galvanize the urban Indian community and reach out to the Indians on the reservations.

We asked for everyone's input and eventually started drawing up a formal plan to use Alcatraz as a cultural center with a vocational training program, an Indian museum, and a spiritual facility. We didn't submit the plan that first year, but over the next several months we refined it. Together we developed our ideas of the practical, historical, and political reasons why Alcatraz should become Indian, and what exactly we would do with it. All of our thoughts were later incorporated into the proclamation made at the takeover, but for the present our plan was simply to make a formal application to the federal government and await their answer.

Then suddenly, two events shoved Alcatraz to the front burner. The first was a vote by the San Francisco Board of Supervisors in favor of preliminary plans for commercial development of Alcatraz submitted by Lamar Hunt of the Texas Hunt family. That came as a bomb shell. There must have been stories in the papers about Hunt's plans, but somehow we missed them. In fact, the first time we heard of his ideas was when the Supervisors voted in their favor.

The implications were enormous. If Hunt's plans succeeded, the federal title to Alcatraz Island would be transferred to private developers. Hunt was reputed to be a billionaire, and he certainly had enough money to accomplish his Texas-size plans to build a huge apartment and restaurant complex on the grounds of the former prison. The whole thing was supposed to be some kind of giant monument to the space age. The idea was that if the East had the Statue of Liberty, the West would have this space-age colossus, complete with an underground space museum. It all sounded very grandiose and unreal, but it was obviously real enough to impress the Board of Supervisors and start them dreaming of new tax revenues rolling in from what was then a white elephant.

But their vote was not yet the final word. Hunt's proposal agitated a lot of non-Indians who were concerned with keeping the bay free of commercial exploitation. The anti-Hunt forces ran a big ad in the local newspapers, complete with a coupon to be filled out by opposed readers. According to the San Francisco papers, the supervisors were inundated with thousands of those coupons protesting the Hunt decision. Yet we had no idea how powerful the commercial forces might be, and we realized that if Hunt went much further, we could kiss our plans for an Indian cultural center goodbye.

A short time later a real calamity befell the San Francisco Indian community. On October 10, 1969, the San Francisco Indian Center on Valencia Street burned down. No cause was ever discovered; it could have been accidental, or it could have been arson. Whatever caused it, the fire was an unmitigated disaster for the Indian people. The Center had been a popular meeting place; an administrative center for all sorts of programs; and a place for social and educational activities, including pow wows. People could socialize with others from their own tribe, find help with their problems, or just get off the streets. There was even a shop that sold Indian arts and crafts.

When the Center went up in flames Indian people throughout the Bay Area mourned it like a close and beloved friend. Everyone asked, "What now? Where do we go?" With outside help, a temporary location was soon established, but it was small and totally inadequate. Something had to be done, and done fast. Alcatraz immediately came to mind.

With the disastrous loss of the Indian Center, the whole emphasis of the Alcatraz discussions shifted from leisurely negotiation to a desire for immediate action. For a year or more we had batted the idea around, gradually moving toward what we considered a reasonable, if idealistic, proposal for federal transfer of Alcatraz to the Indian people. In early September of 1969 we were still talking about proposals and applications. When we first heard about Hunt's grandiose plans, we realized that there was no way we could counter his proposal with just another proposal. He had the money and the political clout, and we had neither. To get anywhere, we would have to develop a different strategy. And then we were confronted with the emergency. There was no way that the Indian people who had relied on the Indian Center would be satisfied with pie-in-the-sky ideas or the slow and unwieldy process of negotiation. They wanted action.

The United Council talked and argued and in the end came down to this: "Take it. Let's do it again, but this time let's do it with sufficient force, and in a way they can't stop. And this time we'll not only take it, but we'll hold it. They won't be able to push us off."

Like distant smoke from a prairie fire, the idea and its potential attracted attention. Our meetings had grown into general gatherings of Indian people, especially since the federal "War on Poverty" had begun in 1964. The programs made no provisions for Indians and left many more frustrated than ever. More people flocked to our meetings. And as

1969 stomped past mid-year with riots in Berkeley and massive, electrifying anti-war protests in San Francisco, Council meetings began to find focus and energy from the restless spirit of more and more young people, many of them college students.

In our enthusiasm we sometimes forgot that Alcatraz was really a cold and desolate place abandoned even as a prison. We forgot because at last we were daring to take back something from all that had been stolen; we would have one isolated place to renew what had been lost. That enthusiastic energy swirled through our meetings, and some on the Council worried that we were being carried away by it and unrealistically riding a dangerous tide of the times. Yet, when each person spoke around the table, the consensus was there—Alcatraz should be ours.

As Chairman of the United Council, it fell to me to conduct the meetings to tentatively determine strategy, a date for the landing, and the wording of the proclamation. When we had made some preliminary plans, I called Don Patterson. Don Patterson was a dapper-dressing Oklahoma native who established his reputation as a southern drum singer while serving as chairman of the San Francisco Indian Center Board of Directors. On behalf of the United Council, I told him of a plan to replace their burned-out building with something bigger and better.

"What? Where?"

"Alcatraz."

Don Patterson then invited me to come and lay out our plans for his board and members. They liked what they heard and agreed to support the occupation and the proclamation.

I next called the chairman of the San Francisco Board of Supervisors to tell him the Indian people did not approve of their plans for the commercialization of Alcatraz. I told him we wanted the island to become an Indian cultural resource. I told him that his Board should be pleased; we could end all the years of agonizing by the white man over the abandoned federal prison. We would buy them out for 24 dollars in beads—exactly the same amount the Dutch paid the Indians for the island of Manhattan. This was clearly a bargain, since Manhattan is several times larger than Alcatraz.

There was an awkward silence on the line. San Francisco politicians pride themselves on knowing the amalgam of ethnic ideals that make up their city and their region. Until then, I had usually been considered among the less threatening of the pressure group leaders.

"Uh, well, yeah, Adam. We could sure think about that," he replied.

Indian students at local colleges, especially San Francisco State, now began to get more involved in the planning. Up until that point, Indian youth had been only sporadically involved in our activities. The Indian students in the United Council had participated when they had time and there was a discussion on issues that directly affected them or their institutions. But with Alcatraz as the catalyst, student input into the Council increased by leaps and bounds until many became actively involved.

Although many people were gung-ho for an Indian Alcatraz and any radical action necessary to achieve that goal, there were still voices of caution and concern. "Do you think we ought to really do something like that? Isn't it too big for us? Is it too hot to handle? What if it gets out of control? What if the federal government uses force? What if somebody gets killed?" Some people worried that an occupation would create more problems than it solved and that it might be too complex for our resources. But when each of us spoke around the table, the consensus was still there. Take the island.

We decided that Alcatraz would definitely replace the Indian Center and thus moved the planning sessions from the United Council meeting rooms to the temporary quarters of the San Francisco Indian Center. I was to be the Council representative at these meetings, although I acted as the chairman of the crucial meeting when we made final decisions on the date of the invasion and the wording of the proclamation.

The interim quarters of the San Francisco Indian Center certainly met our needs. So different from the former center, a gloomy meeting hall inherited from some forgotten Masonic Lodge, the temporary center was a ground floor storefront in the Mission District. Huge show windows looked into a yawning empty room the size of a five-and-dime. There were no chairs, but nobody seemed to mind standing. Those long chilly meetings were warmed with bodies crowded into the unheated display room.

Some of the college students suggested waiting until Christmas to invade, in order to avoid disrupting classes and thus assure a larger student participation. I saw their point, but I knew that if we were going to do it at all, it should be done as soon as possible. We had to move before plans to exploit the island had gone any further and before the authorities could take steps to prevent any kind of landing. I also knew of some really big anti-Vietnam War rallies being planned for December. If they happened at the same time as our takeover, they would probably overshadow us in the media and thus ruin what we were trying to accomplish.

I proposed November 9 as the day of the invasion. That wouldn't give us much lead time, but it also wouldn't give the government a lot of time to snoop out our plans and throw us a curve. I also pointed out that the news was so dull the papers were reduced to printing boring stuff that would normally have landed in the wastebasket.

"You know it has to be a pretty slow time for news," I said, "for the media to be printing speeches by Spiro Agnew. We have to take advantage of that. We need to strike soon, the sooner the better, to get maximum exposure."

So we agreed that November 9, 1969, was Indian D-Day. The rest of our plans were still vague because we realized we could only plan so far. We had so many fine ideas and ideals, but we also realized that many of our actions would be determined by reactions from the federal authorities. We had no way of knowing what those reactions might be, but throughout all this preparation, the possibilities never left our minds.

We constantly stressed that this invasion would be peaceful, just like the Sioux invasion back in 1964. Non-violence was the overriding watchword—non-violence, no liquor, and no drugs of any kind. We were going to be a positive example for Indian people and show a positive face to the world.

The question of who, or what group, would represent the Indian people had already been much discussed in our United Council meetings, and it was now an active topic of discussion at the chilly storefront in San Francisco. Everyone agreed that we wanted to promote a movement rather than any one individual. Secondly, because we also did not want to promote any one tribe, we wanted to find some designation that would proclaim our unity. The 1964 invasion had been an exclusively Sioux action because it took place under the terms of the Sioux Treaty of 1868, but this was different. This protest involved people from many Indian nations. Tlingit, Iroquois, Blackfoot, Chippewa, Navajo, and virtually every other Native American tribe was represented among the thousands of Indians in the Bay Area. Finally, we agreed on a name we could use to structure the occupying force and sign the proclamation—"Indians of all Tribes." We then all agreed that our proclamation should be a mixture of humor, serious intentions, and hope. But the humor should not be just the laughing kind; it should also have a sting.

After these decisions were made, all our preparations were squeezed into a very narrow time frame. The Center had burned down on October 10. The first landing on Alcatraz was set to take place less than a month later on November 9. During those few weeks, there would be a crucial discussion with a young student leader named Richard Oakes and an announcement to the media to prepare for something big in the Indian community.

THE MESSAGE

As we continued to discuss the proclamation, there was a flood of suggestions about what to say in this historic document. Many of the ideas were good ones, and the final proclamation reflected this involvement. But we hadn't yet learned that the media and the public have very short attention spans: if you want a message to sink, in it has to be short and to the point. However true or important the words might have been, most of the final proclamation never made it onto the air or into print. For the record, here it is:

> To the Great White Father and All His People:
> We, the native Americans, re-claim the land known as Alcatraz Island in the name of all American Indians by right of discovery. We wish to be fair and honorable in our dealings with the Caucasian inhabitants of this land, and hereby offer the following treaty: We will purchase said Alcatraz Island for 24 dollars ($24) in glass beads and red cloth, a precedent set by the white man's purchase of a similar island about 300 years ago. We know that $24 in trade goods for these sixteen acres is more than was paid when Manhattan Island was sold, but we know that land values have risen over the years. Our offer of $1.24 per acre is greater than the 47¢ per acre the white men are now paying the

California Indians for their land. We will give to the inhabitants of this land a portion of that land for their own, to be held in trust by the American Indian Government—for as long as the sun shall rise and the rivers go down to the sea—to be administered by the Bureau of Caucasian Affairs (BCA). We will further guide the inhabitants in the proper way of living. We will offer them our religion, our education, our life-ways, in order to help them achieve our level of civilization and thus raise them and all their white brothers up from their savage and unhappy state. We offer this treaty in good faith and wish to be fair and honorable in our dealings with all white men.

The "Bureau of Caucasian Affairs" was, of course, meant to be a dig at the Bureau of Indian Affairs, although during the course of the occupation the BCA became something entirely different from what we had in mind. In the next section of the document we used gallows humor and a little tongue-in-cheek exaggeration to make some important points we wanted the government and the public to take to heart:

We feel that this so-called Alcatraz Island is more than suitable as an Indian Reservation, as determined by the white man's own standards. By this we mean that this place resembles most Indian reservations, in that:

1. It is isolated from modern facilities, and without adequate means of transportation.

2. It has no fresh running water.

3. The sanitation facilities are inadequate.

4. There are no oil or mineral rights.

5. There is no industry and so unemployment is very great.

6. There are no health care facilities.

7. The soil is rocky and non-productive and the land does not support game.

8. There are no educational facilities.

9. The population has always been held as prisoners and kept dependent upon others.

*Further, it would be fitting and symbolic that ships
from all over the world, entering the Golden Gate,
would first see Indian land, and thus be reminded of
the true history of this nation. This tiny island would
be a symbol of the great lands once ruled by free and
noble Indians.*

Then we got to the heart of the matter: the way we wanted to use
Alcatraz if we could persuade the government to turn it over to us. There
was nothing funny about this; it was all very straightforward. If in retrospect our idealism surpassed our sense of the possible, I think we can
be forgiven. In those days we really thought almost anything was possible if we just tried hard enough and got enough people on our side. If
I felt some gnawing doubts in the back of my mind, I sure didn't let them
bother me.

The most important thing was to establish the clear-cut conflict
between what Indians needed and the present plans for the exploitation
of the island. We were partially successful; at least Alcatraz didn't become some real estate speculator's private domain and source of fat profits.
This section of the proclamation was entitled, "Use To Be Made Of
Alcatraz Island":

*What use will we make of this land? Since the San
Francisco Indian Center burned down, there is no
place for Indians to assemble. Therefore, we plan to
develop on this island several Indian institutions:*

*1. A Center for Native American Studies will be
developed which will train our young people in the
best of our native cultural arts and sciences, as well
as educate them in the skills and knowledge to
improve the lives and spirits of all Indian peoples.
Attached to this Center will be traveling universities,
managed by Indians, which will go to the Indian
Reservations in order to learn from the people the
traditional values which are now absent from the
Caucasian higher educational system.*

*2. An American Indian Spiritual Center will be
developed which will practice our ancient tribal
religious ceremonies and medicine. Our cultural arts
will be featured and our young people trained in
music, dance, and medicine.*

3. An Indian Center of Ecology will be built which will train and support our young people in scientific research and practice in order to restore our lands and waters to their pure and natural state. We will seek to de-pollute the air and the water of the Bay Area. We will seek to restore fish and animal life, and to revitalize sea life which has been threatened by the white man's way. Facilities will be developed to desalt sea water for human use.

4. A Great Indian Training School will be developed to teach our peoples how to make a living in the world, improve our standards of living, and end hunger and unemployment among all our peoples. This training school will include a Center for Indian Arts and Crafts, and an Indian restaurant serving native foods and training Indians in culinary arts. This Center will display Indian arts and offer the Indian foods of all tribes to the public, so that all may know of the beauty and spirit of the traditional Indian ways.

5. Some of the present buildings will be taken over to develop an American Indian Museum, which will depict our native foods and other cultural contributions we have given to all the world. Another part of the Museum will present some of the things the white man has given to the Indians, in return for the land and life he took: disease, alcohol, poverty and cultural decimation (as symbolized by old tin cans, barbed wire, rubber tires, plastic containers, etc.). Part of the Museum will remain a dungeon, to symbolize both those Indian captives who were incarcerated for challenging white authority, and those who were imprisoned on reservations. The Museum will show the noble and the tragic events of Indian history, including the broken treaties, the documentary of the Trail of Tears, the Massacre of Wounded Knee, as well as the victory over Yellow-Hair Custer and his Army. In the name of all Indians, therefore, we re-claim this island for our Indian nations, for all these reasons. We feel this claim is just and proper, and that this land should rightfully be granted to us for as long as the rivers shall run and the sun shall shine.

The proclamation was signed with the words, "INDIANS OF ALL TRIBES, November 1969, San Francisco, California."

It seems we should have known that none of this would come to pass, no matter how much truth and justice we had on our side. For one thing, where would we get the money for all of these plans? Desalinization plants? Museums? And we were talking about tens of millions of dollars. All for Indians? Even then, in our heart of hearts, maybe we knew that Alcatraz would never be what we planned. Or maybe we felt that if we expressed extravagant hopes and made extravagant demands, some part of them, however modest, might become a reality. Nothing could make things worse than they already were for Indian people. Besides, compared to what Indians have lost since the coming of the white man, no demand for redress can be considered extravagant—unrealistic, perhaps, but not extravagant.

Once we had agreed upon the action and the proclamation we set about involving the media. We already had one good contact. Tim Findley, a young reporter for the *San Francisco Chronicle*, had become a friend of my family. (Later on Tim even became our adopted son.) He had a strong interest in the urban Indians—Indians were his "beat"—and he eventually covered the Alcatraz story from beginning to end. We told Tim that there was something coming down in the Indian community, something big and newsworthy. Could he suggest a way to announce it to the media? A press conference, perhaps? Would anyone but himself come to a press conference called by a bunch of Indians?

"It so happens I am giving a party for some media people at my house," he said, "and that might be a good opportunity for you. I'm also thinking of inviting Richard Oakes and his wife, Ann, if that's fine with you. But other than that, you and Bobbie will be the only Indian people there."

This was a better opportunity than we had dared hope for. I accepted, of course. I felt that inviting Richard, an activist student leader at San Francisco State, was a great idea. It was also a lucky break for me, because I wanted to sound him out. I hoped to get him involved in something bigger than his Indian student group, something involving a large part of the Bay Area Indian community.

Yet I was really anxious about approaching Richard, a husky, handsome, young Mohawk with a shock of thick black hair. Richard was of the younger generation, and Indian people felt some of the same alienation between the young and the old that white society felt in those days. Young Indians felt particularly removed from those of us who had moved into a more privileged economic status. I wanted to find out for myself what kind of real leader Richard could be, and the best place to do that was away from other young activists who might expect him to be adversarial. Hopefully, the party would be the place. We were looking for somebody to lead the charge, but I wanted to feel sure that Richard was the right man.

Richard and I might have had comparable blue-collar backgrounds, but we seemed to be worlds apart. I was over 40 at a time when the prevailing slogan was "never trust anyone over 30." I had been out of Indian school for more than 20 years and had become a well-off independent businessman, with a nice house and expensive car. Richard was a much younger man, an activist student leader who came from the dangerous and risky world of high steel. He was certainly much closer than I to the typical hand-to-mouth existence of minority students in California. Our differences were intensified by my status as a faculty member in the same state college system where he was a student. (I taught at Cal State Hayward in the East Bay, where I was a part-time instructor in Native American cultures.) I couldn't blame Richard if he thought that since I had more to lose, I was less prone to take risks—in other words, that I might be (God forbid) a moderate. I may have been a moderate, although I considered myself a non-violent activist.

In any event, we did have something in common to bridge the gulf between us: a deep concern with the Indian cause. We both believed in an Indian Alcatraz, at least then, and we were both family men. Richard and his wife had five children, ranging in age from two to twelve, so we both had a big personal stake in the future.

When we arrived at the party at Tim Findley's house, I told Richard of our plans. He jumped at the idea and quickly responded, "Yeah, let's take it."

Forget the discussions, the agonizing, the sleepless nights, the nagging doubts, the pressure from events over which we had no control. That was all in the past. There was never any doubt in Richard's mind, none of the hesitation that comes with age—and to be honest, with more to lose.

"You going to lead the charge?" I asked.

"Okay," he replied. That clinched it.

The decision to go ahead was now irreversible. We called Tim over and told him first, because he was our host and a reporter involved with the urban Indian story.

"Man," he exclaimed, "that's going to be one hell of a story."

Of course, he wasn't completely surprised. He knew there was something big in the works, something radical we had up our sleeves. He also knew that it had to do with Alcatraz. He had known all along what was happening at the United Council and the temporary Indian Center; we had talked about Alcatraz and its pros and cons for more than a year. As a reporter on a big city daily, especially a reporter with a strong interest in Indian activities, he wanted a real story as much as we wanted to stop being invisible. And this was sure one *real* story.

I did have one concern. We didn't want it to appear that a member of the media had actually been in on the planning and was being rewarded by exclusive access to the story.

"No danger of that," Tim assured me. He pointed out that he was getting the full story at exactly the same time as his colleagues, some of whom certainly knew that something was bound to happen with Alcatraz sooner or later. He would also have to observe restrictions on the story's release like everyone else. Tim nodded to me, "Go ahead and make your speech."

Several reporters from the Bay Area papers and radio and television stations gathered around. I gave them a bit of the history of the Alcatraz action and then outlined our plans. I told them a proclamation of the Indian plans for Alcatraz was in the works. It was self-explanatory and would be handed out to them and read aloud on the day of the big event—November 9, 1969—and not before. I warned them that if any one of them broke the story in advance there would be no story.

"In other words," I emphasized, "if the story breaks before November 9, there will be no Indian takeover of Alcatraz. We will simply call it off. Please respect our confidence and trust." And they did. Not one of them so much as hinted at the takeover before it happened.

Thus it was that the Bay Area media were tipped off to what we called the "takeover" and what later became known as the "Indian invasion of Alcatraz." This involvement paid off later. Since we supplied the media with some essential background beforehand, we really did get more complete coverage than many of us expected from the establishment media.

THE FIRST ATTEMPT

As D-Day approached, the meetings and telephone calls became increasingly urgent. I almost totally ignored my own business while I scrambled to persuade and negotiate, tripping over a rumor here and a ruffled ego there. Many questions and issues came up. One person would speak to another and that would lead to a telephone call to someone else and then to a club meeting which in turn called for another full gathering of the Council. People wanted to know what to wear, what they could do with their kids, where they could park, and what would happen if we were arrested.

As always, there were uneasy rumblings about tribal differences and who would be seen as the leader. Nervous planning sessions often evolved into discussions of who would be blamed for failure as well as who would claim credit for success. At least there was general agreement that I, as the Council's elected chairman, could most likely be blamed for whatever might wrong.

The first order of business was to secure transportation. We contacted several charter boat outfits and told them only that as a group of Indians planning an outing to Alcatraz we needed several good-sized boats. That wasn't a lie—we really were planning an "outing." What we didn't add was that not everyone who sailed to the island intended to return. Five skippers agreed, and we were elated. Five boats were enough to transport the 75 Indian people who were eager to be in the first wave of occupants. Pier 39 was our point of embarkation, and we had notified the media accordingly.

The weather on Sunday morning, November 9, 1969, was beautiful and calm, just the kind of day we had hoped for. My family and I set out from our home in San Leandro. We had our tribal outfits packed and the $24 in beads and colored cloth already arranged in a wooden bowl for the symbolic purchase of the island from the government. Feeling optimistic, we were soon on the Nimitz Freeway heading for Fisherman's Wharf and Pier 39 in San Francisco. I began thinking that we were doing a pretty strange thing. 20th-century urban Indians who had gathered in tribal councils, student organizations, and clubs. were now gathering with concerned individuals from all over the Bay Area to launch an attack on a bastion of the United States Government. Instead of riding horses and carrying bows, arrows, and rifles, we were riding in Fords, Chevys, and Plymouths and carrying only our proclamation and determination to change the federal policy oppressing our people.

We paid our 50 cents to cross the Bay Bridge and even got a friendly wave from the toll collector as we continued on our way, taking in the beauty of the scene. Ahead on our right lay Treasure Island, and we could see the Golden Gate further across the bay on the western horizon. South of the bridge lay the sprawl of the city of San Francisco, and to the north rose the purplish hills of Marin County, with Angel Island snuggled up to its shore. Amidst all this natural and man-made beauty sat the forlorn and neglected little island of Alcatraz—our destination.

We were excited, but there was still room for reason, tension, and anxiety. I knew the risks we were about to take; if things went wrong, I could personally lose a lot. I had made a strong commitment to my people, but if things backfired I could be virtually exiled. I certainly wouldn't become involved in more Indian programs for the community, because by tradition Indians who brought dishonor and embarrassment to their people were banished. If things went wrong on Alcatraz, the blanket would be split. I thought about that a lot. I also thought of the other parts of my life, my business and my obligations to my family. What if there was violence? What if I went to jail?

I was also worried about the media. Would we get decent coverage? And what if things went wrong? The media could subject us to public ridicule and scorn, a situation the Indian people certainly didn't need. Finally, I worried about the federal government. We had thought a lot about their reaction to an Indian protest of this kind, but we could only speculate what they would do to us. After all, Indian people had been killed for a lot less in the old days, and we hadn't seen much change in attitude or policy in recent times.

We were nearing Fisherman's Wharf; smells of the delicious seafood for which the wharf is famous filled the air. As we pulled up to the dock we could see several Indians and a couple of television crews milling around. We were greeted by shouts. "Where the hell are the boats?" The first sign of trouble.

As calmly as possible I replied, "They are supposed to be over by the Harbor Tours dock. There should be about five of them."

"Nope. There ain't a damn thing there next to the wharf except the Harbor Tours boat. The bastards must've chickened out!" They sure had. Everyone was worried and angry.

Another worried voice exclaimed, "Jesus Christ! We've got to find ourselves a boat or we're in big trouble with the press—those guys will tear us up!"

I hurriedly parked the car and ran over to the growing group of Indian students. I asked them to keep everyone occupied by stalling for time any way they could while we went looking for another boat. Richard Oakes asked if they could read the Proclamation; it would take a bit of time and he felt the need for more participation by the students from San Francisco State. I handed him a copy.

He and his group set out for the end of the pier, the other Indians and the television crews following. The students settled down in a clearing of benches and planters with Alcatraz Island as a hazy backdrop—a perfect setting for an outdoor press conference. With that diversion begun, we directed our attention to finding a boat.

I telephoned a bait shop which I knew had a fleet of party boats used in deep-sea salmon fishing, and the shop gave me the name and number of a skipper. I reached him on the first try and explained our situation. He asked for $50—double what the Indians got for Manhattan. When I told him that was fine he assured me he would be right down to the dock. We hurried back to the pier where the press conference was in full swing.

The reporters took notes while three different Indians read the three main sections of the proclamation aloud. When they finished, we began singing and dancing so the media would have some action to tape. Tim Findley approached me and asked if there was a problem; it was becoming apparent that we were stalling. I quickly explained our predicament. He felt that if we didn't get something started quickly the whole thing would be treated as a joke, and we'd be in big trouble. "You know, 'Indian time' and all that," Tim confided. I assured him we were very much aware of the problem, but we had the skipper's promise of a boat. I asked the whereabouts of the reporter from Reuters who had faithfully promised to show up. He pointed toward "the Rock."

"See that boat sitting off to the side of Alcatraz? That's where he's at, along with a photographer and a television crew. They want to catch the actual landing. That's what I mean when I say you'll be in big trouble if this doesn't come off."

I left Tim to check on the boat. It was still tied to the dock with no skipper in sight. This is no way to launch an attack, I thought, just too damn complicated. How much nicer in the old days! First there was a big pow wow. Warriors prepared themselves for battle by taking purifying sweat baths and then gathering their personal medicine to ward off enemy bullets or arrows. They made offerings and prayers to their protector before joining the war dance. Oh, the songs and dances were thrilling to behold: as the dancing went on the tempo of the drum increased and its sound grew louder and louder, adding to the fervor. Dancers acted out what they intended to do to the enemy...

I brought myself back to reality and wondered what our next move should be if the skipper didn't show up at all—and it was becoming increasingly evident that this might be the case. As I stood on the wharf I watched a beautiful three-masted barque that looked like it had come right out of the pages of maritime history. It was named the *Monte Cristo*. I watched the crew members go about their tasks under the observant eye of a handsome man with an air of authority. He had to be either the captain or the owner. From a distance, his tight pants, ruffled shirt, and long blond hair made him look like Errol Flynn in an adventure movie. I later learned that his name was Ronald Craig and he was the owner of the beautiful vessel.

Still wearing my full tribal dress, I began to approach him. He called over to me, "Hey, I'm curious. What's going on over there with all those Indians?" I didn't hesitate for a minute, because I realized he could be our solution. I explained our predicament and pointed out the sizeable media contingent that had now gathered. He gave it all a moment of thought. Then he started asking questions that showed concern and sympathy for Indian people and their problems. I kept wondering if his concern was genuine, until finally I could hold back no longer and asked if he could take us to Alcatraz on his beautiful boat.

He stood deliberating this request. He looked at the whole scene: a growing crowd of Indian men, women and children, all wearing different tribal outfits; the news media with their paraphernalia; and curious bystanders and tourists who waited out of curiosity for something to happen. He looked at his ship, then looked again at the Indians. I held my breath. Finally he spoke.

"I'll do it on the condition that we get permission from the Coast Guard to put out to sea and that we take no more than 50 people aboard. The boat rides deep in the water because of the keel, so I can't land on the Alcatraz dock. We'll just circle the island a couple of times, if that's all right with you. Just a sort of sight-seeing tour to get your message across, okay?"

Was it okay? Man alive! At this point I was ready to accept a kayak and he wanted to know if his offer was okay!

I ran back to the wharf to share the good news. Worried looks quickly turned into big smiles as word spread among the Indians and here and there a whoop of joy went up from the crowd.

In a rush, we all converged on the *Monte Cristo*. In no time her decks were awash with Indians, reporters, photographers, and even some of the curious bystanders who came along for whatever adventure lay ahead. But we quickly realized that we had far more than 50 people. Captain Craig approached me shaking his head.

"We can't shove off with this many people aboard," he warned, "the Coast Guard will never let us cast off at this rate. "We took a head count and then started the unpleasant task of asking people to leave the boat. The media people had to stay because without them much of our plans and efforts would be wasted. If nobody could read about our action or watch it on television, it might as well never have happened. As somebody once said: if a tree falls in the forest and there's no one to hear it crash, does it make any sound? Besides, the media had shown exceptional patience and forbearing. So we considered safety and politely asked everyone who could not swim, especially the young children and the older people, to leave the boat.

We immediately felt sorry. The expressions of the elders told all too plainly the deep hurt they felt at being left behind. They had waited a lifetime for Indian people to assert themselves and reclaim their pride. They now stood in somber silence, some with misty eyes—oh, to be young again and have the vigor and strength of the students!

There was one old Dakota Sioux who had told me earlier why he wanted so much to be part of this action. For him, he said, it would be a small revenge for what had happened to his people back in 1890 at Wounded Knee. During the massacre (the Army called it a battle, but the Indians called it what it was, an unprovoked massacre of their men, women and children), his father, then a small child, had huddled in his family's tepee while dozens of bullets splattered through its thin buffalo hide walls. His grandfather had gone out to call for peace, but he was shot down by the men of the 7th Cavalry. His grandmother ran out to the side of her mortally wounded husband and she too was killed— another soldier charging on horseback through the center of the camp ran a sabre into her body.

I thought about that as I watched him slowly leave the *Monte Cristo* and return to the dock. He stood watching with clear disappointment on

his face. Many elders left the boat in silence. But the children were outraged at being left behind, and they loudly let us know their feelings in
no uncertain terms. Yet orders were orders, and if we were ever going to
push off from the dock Captain Craig's request had to be honored.

When he had satisfied himself that there were about 50 people left
aboard he ordered the crew to cast off all the lines. The *Monte Cristo*
had a small cannon mounted on the bow, and one of the crew set it off
with a terrific blast. What a romantic gesture! The crew worked with
well-trained precision, and we were soon underway. People on the dock
waved and cheered, while amateur and professional photographers caught
the symbolic moment.

What a strange turnabout of history, I thought. Here were nearly 50
Indians on an old sailing vessel, heading out to seek a new way of life for
their people. I thought of the *Mayflower* and its crew of Pilgrims who
had landed on our shores 350 years earlier. The history books say they
were seeking new freedom for themselves and their children, freedom
denied them in their homeland. It didn't matter that Plymouth Rock
already belonged to somebody else; that was not their concern. What did
concern them was their own fate and their own hopes. What a sad com-
mentary on this country that we, the original inhabitants, were forced to
make a landing 350 years later on another rock, the rock called Alcatraz,
to focus national attention on our struggle to regain that same basic
freedom.

Yet we were in a festive mood as the barque made its way across the
bay to Alcatraz. Several Indians had set a large drum on the roof of the
captain's quarters, and they were pounding the drum and singing war
dance songs. Alcatraz loomed ever larger straight ahead, and the photographers were all over the place trying to get Alcatraz and the Indians
in their colorful dress into the same picture.

It felt wonderful to ride on that beautiful vessel slicing through the
water to the sound of the Indian drum and war songs, listening to the
laughter and the excited chatter about what lay ahead. The boats on
either side of us were loaded with the camera crews from several television stations and reporters from the local papers and the wire services—
Associated Press, United Press International, and Reuters. Pleasure boats
filled with curious onlookers joined the group and its celebratory spirit.

Then, God forbid, a Coast Guard cutter appeared, approaching with
more speed than any of the other boats. Worried looks and exclamations
replaced the laughter.

"You think somebody tipped them off?"

"If we get turned around now we don't have a chance!"

The Coast Guard cutter continued coming straight toward us.

"Wave at them, smile at them, keep waving!" I shouted to the people near me, and the word spread rapidly. The cutter came closer. We could see its men staring with amazement at our stately old three-master with its owner dressed as a buccaneer and the decks filled with singing, smiling, waving Indians in tribal garb. This bizarre scene proved contagious. Pretty soon the entire crew of the Coast Guard vessel was responding with waves and smiles. We broke out with cheers of relief as the cutter veered away and continued on whatever mission it had interrupted in order to get a gander at us.

The *Monte Cristo* headed for the west side of Alcatraz. There it was with its catwalks and huge walls topped with coiled barbed wire. The old guard towers, now silent and empty, stood as grim sentinels of the island's famous and horrific past. As we drew closer, we could see that the steel ramps and catwalks had rusted from the corrosive salt water air; they were buckled and broken into grotesque shapes. The empty machine shops and laundry facilities came into view as we rounded the northwest corner of the island. Abandoned and rusting equipment sat forlornly everywhere we looked. I thought of how beautiful the island must have been before the white man came to it and left part of his culture and its ugliness.

My somber thoughts were suddenly interrupted by an unexpected drama on the ship—Richard Oakes had climbed onto the railing, stripped off his shirt, and plunged into the water, still wearing his boots! A cheer went up from the Indians as they jammed against the rail. One of the students followed Richard into the frigid waters, and then another! Three Indians were swimming toward the island as hard and fast as they could before the captain had a chance to react. But react he did, and in no uncertain terms.

"What the hell are those guys doing, Adam?" he shouted to me.

"They're swimming to Alcatraz," I replied as calmly as possible.

"What the hell for?"

"To take the island for the Indian people."

"Jesus Christ, man," shouted Captain Craig, "don't you realize we are flying the Canadian flag? This could be considered an act of war! You've got to stop them!"

Somebody, probably a crew member, thrust a bullhorn at me. "Tell them that by order of the captain everybody has to stay put. No more jumping overboard." I couldn't argue with that; the captain is the boss on a ship. I pressed the trigger of the horn to make the announcement.

"The captain has just instructed me to relay his orders. No more Indians are to jump overboard. It is the captain's orders. I am giving you his words—no more Indians are to jump overboard!"

The immediate response was a loud splash as another Indian took a flying leap over the side. Everyone cheered except an Eskimo named Joe Bill, who was wise to the ways of the sea. He stood shaking his head, "No good, no good." We would soon understand his words.

The captain was really panicked now; people just don't jump off ships that are underway. He had a boat full of eager Indians cheering for four of their brothers splashing their way through the frigid waters toward Alcatraz. He kept an anxious watch for the next man to jump overboard.

We all began to see what Joe Bill had seen earlier: the tide was flowing in the wrong direction for the swimmers and sweeping them out to the Golden Gate, instead of towards Alcatraz. As the ship continued toward the eastern side of Alcatraz the sweep of the tide grew more favorable. Without another word to me Joe Bill quickly stripped off his shirt and shoes. Just as the captain noticed and rushed towards him, Joe Bill plunged over the side. Again, cheers rose from the Indians remaining on deck. We all watched Joe make remarkable progress toward Alcatraz, unlike the other jumpers. In what seemed a matter of moments he had reached the island, scrambled up on the craggy shore, turned, and waved at us with a big smile. More cheers went up for him—Indians were on Alcatraz once again! The drum started pounding victory songs and everybody gave loud cheers and war whoops.

The captain issued orders for the helmsman to swing wide of the island to discourage any more leaps onto the water. The *Monte Cristo* made its final turn and headed back toward San Francisco. Although only one Indian swimmer had made the landing on Alcatraz, we had achieved at least a token victory. We had escaped from a potential fiasco with the press and given hope to our people. But was this enough? I still had the bullhorn, and with it I called to the group.

"Have we done enough?"

There was a loud chorus. "NO!"

"Do you want to go back and take Alcatraz? Really take it?"

"Yes! Let's go!" came the ready answer, with war whoops added for emphasis.

"All right," I answered. "When we get back to the wharf, spread the word that we'll meet at the Indian Center."

When we arrived at the dock, our swimmers were already on land, shivering in the cold November air. They had been picked up and returned by friendly boaters and news crews; even Joe Bill had been rescued. One jumper was throwing up a good amount of salt water he had swallowed during his swim. By this time, it was late afternoon and we were all hungry; we hadn't had a chance to eat since morning. I figured that buying lunch for the courageous swimmers was a small enough contribution on my part. My good feeling ebbed away a bit when I saw at least 50 hungry Indians line up behind the swimmers at a nearby stand. Hamburgers, hot dogs, clam chowder, cokes, and floats were served at a fast clip. Bobbie gave me a silent look, but she dug into her purse and handed me some money. Half an hour and $48.00 later, we had finished our lunch and were ready to set out for the temporary Indian Center in San Francisco.

Indian people of all ages and tribes were already jammed into the building when we arrived. Everyone was discussing the events of the day. We found the same consensus we had found on the *Monte Cristo*: everyone wanted to go back that very night and land in force on the island. Since we had pulled quite a few rabbits out of the hat that day and luck seemed to be going our way, I tried to locate another boat. One of my brothers once worked as a skipper for some of the deep-sea fishing parties that set out regularly from San Francisco, and I had met some of the guys he worked with. A few phone calls proved our luck was indeed still holding out.

NIGHT LANDING

I talked to the captain of a deep-sea fishing boat called the *New Vera II* that had just docked at the wharf; her crew was still washing down the deck. He agreed to take us out to the island if we guaranteed him a minimum payment of $50.00 or $3.00 per person. I didn't even try to bargain. After the problems we'd had finding boats, I couldn't risk letting this one get away. Some of our people called it a white man's scalping, but beggars can't be choosers. The captain told me we had to move out within half an hour because he had another appointment. I announced this immediately, and people quickly began gathering up their sleeping bags and blankets and ensuring that everyone had enough money for passage.

Once again we headed for Fisherman's Wharf, but things were different when we arrived in the growing dusk. There were no press people, no curious bystanders, no tourists, and only a small band of Indians. We walked with an air of secrecy past Castagnola's Restaurant, the boats lying waiting for repairs, and the reeking fish containers until we found the *New Vera II*. She was sitting almost out of sight across from Scoma's Restaurant, her deck still wet and glistening from her recent scrubbing.

The captain was waiting for us on board and he shouted up to us, "Hurry up you guys, we've got to get going!"

Several people scrambled down the steel ladder on the side of the dock and jumped down to the deck. They were followed by a shower of sleeping bags and blankets.

"Anybody got the chow?" somebody wanted to know.

"No, I thought you had it."

"Nope."

"Hey, anyone up there got any food for us to take with us?" A few loaves of sourdough bread flew down from the small cluster of Indians on the dock.

"That's all we got, guys."

The diesel engine came to life and we took a quick head count. Richard Oakes was missing.

"We can't go without him," someone yelled. "Where the hell is he? God damn, we can't go on Indian time now!"

The captain was getting impatient.

"Look," he warned, "I told you I'd give you half an hour, and we're already overdue. Five more minutes, that's all you have. Make up your minds. Go without him or not at all."

We stationed lookouts at the front of the dock to check for latecomers. The five minutes raced by, and the skipper gave orders to cast off the lines. The engine revved, and the boat began to edge out from the dock.

"Hey! Hey!"

We could hear footsteps on the dock; somebody was running on the opposite side of the marina. It was Richard and a few others, running and shouting to get our attention. They had gone to the wrong dock and hadn't been able to find us. "Hey, captain," I shouted, "back this tub up and let's load these guys aboard." He responded by throwing the gears into reverse.

All our noise and shouting brought someone to the window of the Coast Guard office directly across the wharf. He stood there looking down at our boat full of Indians as Richard and the others scrambled aboard with their sleeping bags under their arms. The phone on the pier started ringing. One of the crew made a start to answer it, but the captain cut him off. "Let it ring, damn it," he snapped, "we've got to get the hell out of here!"

He opened the throttle of the *New Vera II* and we slipped out into the bay for the second time that day, only this time we slipped into the gathering darkness. Of the 200 or so Indians who had been prepared to assault the island that sunny afternoon, there were no more than 25 of us on the voyage of the *New Vera II*.

"Christ, it's cold tonight," shivered Earl Livermore, former director of the San Francisco Indian Center and a member of the Blackfoot tribe. We clasped our jackets tightly around us; others wrapped themselves in blankets to ward off the damp and chilly wind that swept over the boat. To make things worse, the water on the wet deck began to soak through the moccasins worn by many of our party. Some went below to escape the cold, including Bobbie and our kids.

Earl and I stayed on deck to watch a scene very different from the one of that morning. We forgot our cold and discomfort as we stared at the magnificent view behind us. San Francisco Bay and the tall buildings of the city were aglow with all kinds of lights—reflected lights, flashing lights, neon lights in red, blue, yellow, and green. The phosphorescent wake of our boat joined this magnificent, almost psychedelic, light show.

It was all so beautiful it was difficult to tear ourselves away and direct our attention to Alcatraz. And what a contrast as we turned to face the island! We just made out its gloomy silhouette against the lights of Richmond and Berkeley before the quick flash of the lighthouse beacon caught our eyes. The underwater cable warning sign glowed with a ghostly bluish light and the mournful moan of the island's two foghorns grew louder as we approached the island. It was hard to decide if the foghorns were there to drive off evil spirits or if Alcatraz itself was the spirit—an evil spirit with a circling cyclops eye and an awful voice sweeping across the waters.

As if to turn us from our goal, the stormy elements completed the dismal picture. The tide was going out, thwarting the captain's attempts to sidle up to the large water barge at the Alcatraz dock. The riptide swirled around our boat, swinging us dangerously about; the lone light on the dock cast only useless eerie shadows. We swung wide to avoid colliding with a barge, circled around, and headed for the boat slip where we had seen the custodian's boat. The captain revved the throttle to help push us into position, but the tide, the darkness, and the unfamiliar dock all kept him from making the landing.

The captain was already getting frustrated when a huge watchdog appeared out of the dark and ran up to our noisy boat barking furiously. Would the caretaker hear the commotion and start shooting as the care-takers used to do when Alcatraz was still a prison? The captain didn't want to stick around long enough to find out. He swung the wheel sharply and headed straight for the barge. "Good God, he's going to ram the damn thing!" someone exclaimed. But at the last moment, the skipper pushed the gears into reverse and the boat gently nudged the barge instead of ramming it. Immediately, people started securing lines and piling over the bow onto the barge. Sleeping bags and blankets were quickly passed along to the dock as we lined up anxiously to disembark.

"Hey, what's going on here?" demanded the skipper. I explained in an off-hand way, "Well, we are going to take over the island."

"Oh my God," he exclaimed, "they might take my boat away for this!"

The captain had been fighting to keep the nose of his vessel against the barge, but he now became completely agitated. Realizing that he could be charged with aiding and abetting our takeover and concerned with the rushing tides and the possibility of being shot any minute by a panicked caretaker, he suddenly threw the gears into reverse once again. The tie line snapped, knocking one of our men back into the boat.

"God damn it," the man hollered, "we aren't even unloaded yet!" But the captain paid no attention as he pushed the throttle wide open to get out of there.

We were disappointed at being left behind on the boat, but we could count fourteen Indians, a sizeable contingent, on the shore of Alcatraz. One was Richard Oakes; three were women. They all flew up the stairway of the old fort and quickly disappeared into the darkness. The watchdog looked on with tail wagging. We joked that our fourteen friends had only two loaves of bread between them, but if they got really hungry they could always cook the dog.

The occupation of Alcatraz Island had become an accomplished fact. What an ironic twist of fate for an old prison island with a grim and sadistic past! In its heyday, desperate men went to any extreme, even certain death, to escape the island. In 1969, Indian people were just as desperate to get on the island to seek freedom.

SPREAD THE WORD

Our trip back to San Francisco was not an idle joy ride. We held a strategy session and agreed that Earl and I would contact the news media to spread the word of the occupation. Earl would call all the radio stations, and I would re-establish contact with the television stations and newspapers. Spread the word: the Indians have taken Alcatraz!

The reaction was immediate, although not without skepticism and disbelief. A reporter from the *San Francisco Examiner* called John Hart, the brusque, barrel-chested Alcatraz caretaker who had once been a guard at the prison and now jealously oversaw its crumbling remains with the aid of his mongrel dog, rumored to be particularly vicious.

"Do you happen to have any Indians out there on the island with you?" inquired the reporter.

"Nope," came the reply, "ain't seen or heard a thing."

"Well," persisted the reporter, "we have some pretty reliable reports that Indians have landed on Alcatraz and taken it over."

"Nope, don't think so, you musta' gotten a crank call."

A few minutes later a reporter called from the *San Francisco Chronicle*. "I have a report that you've got some Indians out on the island. Do you know if this is true?"

Hart's patience was wearing thin. "There ain't no damned Indians out here!"

The reporter responded with another question about the landings that afternoon by the Indian swimmers.

"I don't like this a damn bit," Hart replied. "It was illegal for them to come on this island. If you saw it you were a party to it and I won't tell you anything more, not even the name of the dog."

With those words, Hart hung up. Now worried that there might just possibly be Indians on the island with him, he grabbed his flashlight and set out on a fruitless search. He knew it probably wasn't true. Still, he had a little nagging doubt—could there really be Indians on Alcatraz?

Meanwhile, the Indians were having their own adventure. Knowing the authorities would not let the occupation go unchallenged, they explored the abandoned prison in the dark, checking it out for hiding places. The top of the island made an incredible vantage point; anything that moved on the water could be easily spotted. The fourteen were especially watchful for anything coming from the direction of the Coast Guard station and Fort Cronkite. The authorities must surely have heard of the landing, and the Indians expected a retaliation.

"Hey, look over there. See it?"

"Yeah, it looks like a Coast Guard cutter. The caretaker must have called them."

It was no mistake—the cutter was heading right toward the island. Although the adventurers weren't sure of it at the time, Hart had indeed phoned the mainland with the report that a bunch of Indians might have landed on the island. The man who took Hart's call at first thought the caretaker was drunk or driven to insanity by the loneliness of Alcatraz— who in their right mind would be seeing Indians running around on Alcatraz?

"How do you know they are Indians? Are they wearing feathers?" he inquired sarcastically. Nonetheless, a Coast Guard cutter was sent to take a look.

The cutter swung broadside 200 yards from the island and sent a finger of light stabbing through the darkness of the prison. To the Indians watching, the slow-moving cutter looked like a mountain lion slowly stalking its prey, yellow eyes peering through the shadows. The cutter first explored the main cell block area, then moved to the warden's house, then slowly searched on down towards the dock. But the light revealed no sign of the Indians, who were careful not to move from their hiding places and expose themselves.

The searchlight moved slowly out of sight as the cutter circled the opposite side of the island. Ten minutes later the ship reappeared on the far side. There had been no signs of any Indians, findings later reported to the newspapers. "Hell, there ain't no Indians out here. This has to be somebody's joke." Some joke!

Much to the relief of the fourteen Indians, the cutter broke off its fruitless search and headed back to home port. Too tense to sleep, some continued to explore the island and stand guard, while others rolled out their sleeping bags and blankets. It was cold, and they huddled together for warmth and comfort to pass the long night ahead.

THE SEARCH

The morning of November 10th greeted the Alcatraz Indians with a scene right out of an old-time Keystone Cop movie. Ships, motorboats, sailing yachts, launches, dinghies, and cutters were all hell bent for Alcatraz. The news was out.

Bold banner headlines and special reports on television and radio spread the word through the Bay Area and beyond. One big, black headline proclaimed boldly, "INDIANS INVADE ALCATRAZ: U.S. PLANS COUNTER-ATTACK!"

On the mainland, Earl Livermore and I stayed on the phone answering questions almost constantly. One wire service reporter found the whole thing hard to believe.

"You mean Indians have really invaded Alcatraz?"

"Yes sir, they sure have."

"How many of them?"

"Fourteen: eleven men and three women."

"Three women? You mean to tell me that there are three women in that invading party and they stayed out there overnight on that miserable island?"

"Yes sir. There would have been more except the rope broke before everybody could get off the boat."

"Good grief! And where will we find them when we get out to the island?"

"I think they'll be a little hard to find," I replied. "If I know that bunch, they'll act like jackrabbits."

Boy, did they ever! A small armada—federal marshals, newspaper reporters, radio and television crews, representatives from the General Services Administration (GSA) which controlled Alcatraz, Coast Guard officials—arrived at the dock of Alcatraz and looked around for some Indians. None were to be seen.

Mr. Hart led the group off in search of the band of occupying Indians. The search party, which far outnumbered the Indian group, trooped up the roadway past the old Alcatraz fort. A mammoth 19th-century structure, its massive eight-foot walls enclosed a network of rooms and passageways with arched doors and windows. High vaulted ceilings and gun emplacements once guarded the bay against invaders. The searchers marched past this fantastic ruin and up the hill toward a curious building with a tunnel running through it. This structure housed a vintage fire engine that still reposed there in the darkness, pretending to be ready just in case duty called.

Fortunately for the Indians, the searchers didn't pause here; if they had they would have been amazed. On closer examination one could see, as the Indians already had, vague traces of an old moat and drawbridge that probably dated back to the island's Spanish past. The drawbridge had been lowered until it sat level with the roadway. When I heard about this, I imagined a conversation between the old relic and the Indians.

"Drawbridge, drawbridge, please come down. We want to walk across you to the other side. We want to walk to freedom."

"And who makes this request?" asked the drawbridge.

"We are fourteen American Indians of all tribes, sir, and we have come to seek freedom for our people."

"This is a prison, not a sanctuary," the drawbridge replied in stern tones. "Besides, this is the 20th century and all people are supposed to be free in this country."

"We know that," the Indians answered. "But we are Indians. Our lands were stolen from us before you even existed. This island was once ours. It was stolen from us. Our self-government, that was stolen. Our beautiful religions were ridiculed and replaced by those of our white conquerors, and our people are now defeated, hungry and poor."

"You are asking far more of this tiny island than it can give to you," said the drawbridge, "but I will do my part for you." With that reply, it slowly lowered itself so that Indians could walk across it toward their distant goal.

But the weary and increasingly frustrated members of the search party missed the drawbridge and continued up the winding road past the warehouse, power plant, machine shops, and laundry facilities. Many of the buildings offered a myriad of hiding places, but none of them revealed any Indians. Finally, the party reached the very top of the island and stood in front of the main cell block with the dungeon buried deep in its bowels.

"Where in hell are we supposed to find those fourteen Indians?" a reporter asked John Hart.

"They could be anywhere, or everywhere."

"There goes one!" A shout went up as a shadowy figure slipped over the top of a concrete stairway and disappeared into the undergrowth covering the area. Television camera operators made off in pursuit, trying their best to run up the same stairs. Their heavy equipment slowed them down, and by the time they reached the top there were no Indians to be seen.

"Where in tarnation did they go?" Hart exclaimed in utter frustration, his hands on his hips and a big frown on his face as a photographer snapped his picture. The search party had missed the fact that the drawbridge had been mysteriously lowered, but they now had visual evidence. So the hunt continued.

Several more hours passed fruitlessly until the Indians decided to end the game of cat and mouse, or cowboys and Indians. They recognized reporter Tim Findley and newscaster Mike Mills and called to them from their hiding places. Everyone in the search party came to a halt. One by one, the fourteen Indians emerged from different buildings scattered in all different directions. Hart and the search party stared in amazement, realizing that the Indians had been accompanying them all along.

The media interviewed the Indians, and then everyone returned to the dock area where Richard Oakes read our Proclamation to the reporters and Thomas Hannon, regional administrator of the GSA. Hannon listened carefully and patiently to each word, but his distress was apparent. When the reading was finished, he told the assembled reporters that if the Indian invaders did not leave peacefully, he would consult with the U. S. Attorney about trespassing charges. He also managed to talk Richard and the thirteen others into temporarily leaving the island so that negotiations might take place in a calmer atmosphere. Then he generously "offered" the Indians a ride back to San Francisco. As they boarded the vessel, Richard Oakes' voice could be heard loud and clear.

"This occupation has established the Indian squatters' right to Alcatraz Island, and we will be back." He then turned to Hannon. "You ready?"

"Let's go," Hannon replied.

The Indians evacuated the island voluntarily in the hope that something could be worked out in accordance with the objectives of the

Proclamation. It soon became apparent, however, that the government was either deliberately dragging its heels or truly unclear on how to proceed. They must have thought, or hoped, that removing the Indians from the island would also remove the problem of what to do with Alcatraz. Perhaps the Indian protest would lose steam, and perhaps the San Francisco Board of Supervisors would somehow resolve the issue.

As a matter of fact, by that time the Board of Supervisors had realized that their vote to accept Lamar Hunt's preliminary plans had stirred up a hornet's nest. The papers were saying that nothing in recent years had created so much controversy and civic opposition. It was hard to say if our actions had any impact on the Board, but they did hold a second meeting at which they reopened the issue of Alcatraz' future. From then on, the Hunt plan was pretty dead in the water. But as far as the Indian demands were concerned, the majority of the supervisors could probably have cared less. We Indians, however, continued to care very much.

In fact, we were getting good and mad at the runaround. We held a number of meetings and decided to go back to the island. This time we were not just going to land and then leave again with some vague government promise to negotiate. This time, we were going to hold onto Alcatraz and force the government to negotiate. We were going to try to make the goals of our Proclamation become realities.

THE TAKEOVER

The day set for the third landing was November 20, 1969. This occupation lasted for nineteen months.

That date happened to overlap with the first National Conference on Indian Education, to which I had been invited in my role as chairman of the United Bay Area Council. It was one or the other for me, Alcatraz or the conference in Minneapolis. I opted for the conference, because it seemed to be a golden opportunity to enlist national Indian support at the very moment when the new occupation was beginning. We held a meeting and discussed the fact that the Minneapolis conference would draw a large number of Indian scholars and tribal leaders. If we could give them firsthand information about our cause, they would take it back to their people. We would gain national support and exposure just when we could use it to our best advantage to put pressure on the government. We all agreed on this strategy.

We needed to have lots of copies of the proclamation to distribute at the conference. We had always had friends in the white community who were willing to do us a good turn with logistical support, and this time was no exception. The Scientific Analysis Corporation of San Francisco jumped into the breach by running off several thousand copies of the four-page proclamation in time for me to take them to Minneapolis.

While there I maintained constant contact with the activities in California. On November 20, I got the message from Bobbie—"The island is being taken again!" I went before a huge assemblage of Indian scholars, educators, and community leaders, and I asked the chairman to recognize me. With the copies of the proclamation under my arm, I explained the purpose of the occupation and asked that they all take copies of the proclamation and share them with their people.

The response was incredible. Cheers broke out as I finished my request, and people crowded around me grabbing for the copies of the proclamation. I could hardly keep up with the demand. Months earlier I had confidently predicted that waves of protest would spread outward from the pebble we tossed into the San Francisco Bay. I had hoped the waves would ultimately reach the national Indian community, and my wishes came true. The conference transformed our remote little Indian activity into a national movement with national support.

The two previous Alcatraz landings also strengthened support for our action. They had captured the imagination of many in the Bay Area, Indians and non-Indians alike. Not only was there considerable sympathy for the Indian cause in the liberal community, but many of the young activists felt excited by the romantic nature of it all.

While I was in Minneapolis, Richard was faced with some problems. He had to gather an occupying force, and he began by appealing to college students. The response was enthusiastic; students came from as far away as Santa Cruz and Los Angeles. Enthusiasm spread until the invasion force of around 90 people included over 30 women, several married couples, and a half dozen young children.

One of the biggest problems was the need for boats. Had Richard been familiar with the spirit of swashbuckling anarchy on the Sausalito waterfront at that time, he might not have needed Tim Findley's help. As it was, one phone call from Tim to Peter Bowen at the No Name Bar set the all-important conspiracy in motion. Peter owned a trim little motor sailer that eventually led the invasion, and two of his friends also possessed power boats and an irreverent spirit.

Chaos reigned supreme that evening, so I can only piece together what happened. I understand that they planned for Richard to have his people filter into Sausalito and arrive in the No Name Bar by closing time at 2 a.m. so they could mingle with the closing crowd. Of course, nobody really "filtered" in, and mingling was absurd to imagine. A troop of 90 gear-laden Indians appeared, mostly at the same time, on the sleepy Sausalito waterfront in the early morning hours of November 20. Peter felt a little alarmed at what he had gotten himself into, but he had committed himself and thus rather grimly set about loading the boats.

Brookes Towns had been sent out earlier in a motorized dinghy to check for lurking Coast Guard vessels. Slightly prone to exaggeration, Brookes very nearly ruined everything when he returned with a hysterical report that the whole island of Alcatraz was lit up like a Christmas tree. Other boatmen determined Brookes had mistaken a working barge out in the bay for the island of Alcatraz, and the boats started on their way.

Except for the light house and a single bulb in the guard shack, the island was dark when the first boat bumped into the dock around 3 a.m. Expecting Hart and his dog, the group was surprised to find a small-framed older man with snow-white hair and bleary eyes. Hart and his dog had gone fishing in the mountains, leaving his assistant, who resembled the character of Ben Gunn from *Treasure Island*, in charge of the whole place. Apparently the noise of the landing awakened him, but when he saw the boats full of Indians he began dancing up and down and shouting, "Mayday! Mayday! The Indians have landed!"

He was right. And they were determined to stay.

The caretaker was Glenn Dodson, a man in his 50s who had taken the job a month before for the "peace and quiet." He directed the Indians to the most comfortable quarters, the three-story frame house that had been the warden's residence.

"I don't really mind," said Dodson to the invaders. "Besides, I'm one-eighth Cherokee myself."

Using remnants of carpet and a few stray pieces of furniture, the Indians quickly set up their headquarters. A fire of junk from the area burned in the fireplace, and a large poster of the Apache chief Geronimo hung above the mantle. The food supply of sandwiches, lots of potato salad, and soft drinks lay on the table. A drum began thumping, and a spontaneous victory pow wow and ceremonial sing began.

At dawn, John Hart returned from his fishing trip to find the fire going and the Indians very awake and still singing. Since Hart had weathered more than 20 years on Alcatraz, the Indians expected him to be confrontational.

"Well, as long as you are here, you might as well be comfortable," Hart told them in a very unfriendly tone. He proceeded to point out the most accessible buildings and those with functional plumbing. Worried about possible injuries, he also warned them of the crumbling walls and catwalks.

The Indians swarmed over the island, checking out the cell blocks, walkways, and other old buildings. This exploration was for both adventure and protection; they would need hiding places if the federal marshals arrived. Before long, big red letters began appearing on the sides of the cement buildings—"You are now on Indian land." The water tower bore its own message: "Peace and Freedom. Welcome. Home of the Free Indian Land." A big warning sign on the south side of the island was altered to read, "Warning. Keep Off Indian Property."

At 4 p.m., General Service Administration's Regional Administrator Thomas Hannon landed on the island with the Indians' two attorneys, Aubry Grossman and R. Corbin Houchins, and a representative from the Department of the Interior. They had been meeting all day with other federal officials. Hannon informed the Indians that if they stayed on the island all their supply boats would be confiscated and they would be arrested.

One hour later, the officials and the Indians reached a compromise. One supply boat would be allowed to land that evening, and a deadline was set for the Indians to leave by noon of the next day. Richard Oakes and four other Indian leaders returned to San Francisco with the Coast Guard to discuss strategy with other Indian representatives. The Indians remaining on the island, fully expecting the government to somehow run them off the island the next day, prepared for a last night on Alcatraz.

"We won't physically resist," said Dennis Turner, a 22-year-old Luiseño, "but how will they find us? It's why we are here in the first place—we are the invisible Americans."

SUPPORT

At the time, no one really understood that the Indians had truly gained possession of "the Rock." Even we didn't understand. The government acted as if it was all just another demonstration by a few more radicals, and the Indians assumed the government would act as always and remove them by force at the deadline. The difference between this invasion and the previous one was that there were now enough Indians on the island and enough support welling up on the mainland to make any government action a major operation. So the government had to take a different tack.

They first attempted to force the Indians out by using the famous Coast Guard blockade, which began almost immediately. Anyone would think that blockading an island in full view of millions of people would be a piece of cake. But the Coast Guard hadn't reckoned on the "pirate" spirit of the boaters of the San Francisco Bay. Especially after the Sausalito crowd went through such heroics to get the Indians to the island, the boaters took it as a challenge to get supplies across as well. Everyone got into the action, whether they used a Chinese junk or a barge.

There is one story of a barge that set out for Alcatraz late one foggy night. One person was left on the mainland to call the news media once the barge landed on the island, which was planned to coincide with the late night news. This person was to be notified of the landing by radio, but radio silence had to be maintained until that time. Time slipped by without word from the barge, until the mainland contact broke the radio silence. There was no reply. Assuming the barge had been stopped, the

Alcatraz Indians receiving supplies. Richard Oakes is second from right. Photo courtesy of the California Historical Society, San Francisco Chronicle Collection, photographer Vincent Maggiora, FN-27948.

person waiting on shore called the news media to tell them the barge had been captured by the Coast Guard. The late night news picked up the story.

The Coast Guard heard the news, and since they had not stopped a barge they went looking for one. They found it, moving more slowly than expected through the thick fog, and made it turn back. The funny thing was that one of the Coast Guard crew told the barge owner, "Hell, we didn't care if you made it through. But when it was announced on the news, we had to come looking for you."

The news media had a heyday with the blockade. One station even set music to the attempts to run the blockade and the Coast Guard attempts to stop them and played the tape on the evening news show. Bay Area residents watched with merriment the television broadcast of an attempt made by a motorized Chinese junk filled with 20 local hippies and some supplies. A Coast Guard cutter headed in to cut the junk off and tie a line to its bow. The junk accidentally rammed the cutter, causing some minor damage, and a lot of chaos. During the confusion two Indians with a small rubber raft hopped off the junk and rowed to the island, setting off a cheer from the people on Alcatraz. The junk then swung around and made a pass by the Alcatraz dock, throwing fruit, a couple of turkeys, milk, and even some beer to the cheering crowd. The humiliated Coast Guard waited until the junk came to shore and then cited the skipper, Peter Jones, for reckless and negligent boat driving.

And the supplies kept coming in. As the Coast Guard blocked the docks on the east side of the island, boats landed on the beach on the west side. Everyone wanted to get in on the action, and Peter Jones received the only citation.

Throughout all this activity, the General Services Administration (GSA) kept in touch with the island. Thomas Hannon, regional director, went out to Alcatraz several times to "negotiate" with the invaders. Hannon did not threaten them with anything worse than the blockade, but he did say that if the demonstrators refused to leave the GSA would take action. He commented, "Ultimately, of course, we'll have to take them off. But I'm in no rush."

The blockade turned out to be a complete failure, and it was lifted three days after it began. We began to see that we really had the island—but now what? When I came back from the conference, the entire Indian community was on fire. There were those who supported the effort, those who were unsure, and there were even Indians who were against the occupation. But one thing was for sure: Alcatraz was on everyone's mind.

With the firestorm of controversy swirling tumultuously about them, more Indians moved onto the island to set up house, sometimes for entire families. Apartments were chosen and the bleak surroundings tidied up as much as possible. Young single Indians took up residence in the main cell block, often using candle smoke to mark their claims on the ceilings of cells once home to America's most hardened and dreaded criminals.

After discovering that there were no sewage facilities on the island, the Indians set up a sanitation program, the first of its kind. Through all the years Alcatraz was used as a fort and a prison, neither the Spaniards nor the U.S. Government had created a disposal system. For more than 125 years, raw sewage and garbage had been dumped directly into San Francisco Bay. Not wanting to pollute the bay, the Indian occupants modified a basement area in one of the old guards' quarters to serve as a type of septic tank.

The first council on Alcatraz was composed of seven young Indians, mostly students. Along with Richard Oakes, there was Al Miller (Seminole) and Ross Harden (Winnebago), students from San Francisco State University; Ed Castillo (Cahuilla), a young professor, and Bob Nelford (Eskimo), a student, both from the University of California at Los Angeles; Dennis Turner (Luiseño) who studied at the University of California at Santa Cruz; and James Baughn (Cherokee), a student from the University of California at Berkeley. This council ran the island in those first few days, but the predominance of students eventually caused some problems. Most of the mainland support came from working Indians, who had a different view of what we were trying to accomplish and the difficulties of turning dreams into reality.

But the first real issue was supplies. The government had abandoned the prison because its upkeep was too costly; they knew all too well the logistical problems we faced. When Thomas Hannon heard of the Indian plans to reclaim the island, he commented that we would have to spend a lot of money. It did cost a great deal of money to secure provisions, but the public support grew as fast as the occupation, much to our relief. Individuals and groups from all over gave their support. Minority groups and churches collected donations; celebrities like Dick Gregory donated money. The folksinger Malvina Reynolds donated money and the royalties of one year from her song, "Alcatraz," about the occupation. Local rock groups immediately began benefit concerts to raise money, and I was asked to speak all over the Bay Area in support of the cause. The word spread like wildfire, much to the government's chagrin.

The Indians' status as "illegal" occupants of an isolated island made it doubly difficult to acquire all the necessities for living. The people maintaining the supply line were the unsung heroes of Alcatraz. It's funny that the people saw only the actual event and the exciting personalities, and missed everything else that went into making the event happen. Like a movie audience that sees only the actors and misses the hundreds of other people that made the movie happen, the public only saw the glamour of the Indians living on the island. Yet much of the credit for the success of the occupation lies with the people who supported it on the mainland. Even the Indians on the island forgot this, and it came to haunt them.

Many of the Indians on the mainland who held jobs or went to school couldn't live on the island. They supported the occupation by working nights or weekends organizing supplies and support, donating money or food, and performing many other hidden tasks. Of course, much credit also goes to the non-Indians who throughout the effort gave generously of food, clothes, equipment, money, and transportation by boat. The boats played a big part in the success of Alcatraz; they helped the Indians thwart government attempts to isolate the island.

One of the truly unsung heroes of Alcatraz was Dr. Dorothy Lone Wolf Miller, a Blackfoot Indian and the director of the Scientific Analysis Corporation that provided much technical support for the occupation. Dorothy opened her offices on California Street in San Francisco for a temporary headquarters for "Indians of All Tribes." She arranged for an account with the Bank of California and helped the Council on Alcatraz set up and maintain their financial books and records. Using her expertise in writing grant proposals, she obtained an education grant to establish a school system on the island in which the Indian women would be the teachers and the formal academic needs of the children would be met.

The island had no running water, heating system, or electricity, but the health needs of the occupants still had to be met. Again, Dorothy Miller responded. She helped set up a health care system equal to that of the city of San Francisco. She brought George Challas, MD, and Jennie Joe, RN, on board to provide basic care. She set up a two-way radio system between Alcatraz and the mainland to facilitate emergency communications; with Peter Blue Cloud manning the radio, a 24-hour communications link was established.

In an effort to expand the coverage of Indian events throughout the country, Dorothy helped establish a newsletter called "Indians of All Tribes News." The members of the editorial board were Peter Blue Cloud, Woesha Cloud North, Young-Robbed-Bird-Free-At-Last, Wolf Running, and Denise Quitiquit. They assembled a small booklet of 20 pages crammed full of Indian issues, concerns, poetry, and announcements of upcoming events. The lines of communication were wide open.

Dorothy Miller tirelessly pursued every possible means to assist in the occupation. Not only did she allow her professional offices on California Street to be used as a mainland headquarters for over four months, but she even allowed Indians to sleep there. She ran a shuttle service of people and supplies to the docks. She donated time, money, professional expertise, and facilities. Her personal modesty would prevent her from claiming any credit, but I know her to be a sincere and dedicated woman. Unfortunately, Dorothy paid a heavy price for her long involvement with the "uprising." As a form of punishment, federal research grants were withheld from her firm for five years, and her personal life suffered as well.

"What the hell!" she exclaimed later. "It was the price I had to pay for freedom!"

I didn't know whether she meant Indian freedom, her own personal freedom, or both. I do know that she now spends a lot of time in old Mexico helping the Indians there.

Not all support was welcomed. Georgia Tachahagachile, who lived on the island for a year, told me a story that went like this:

"One day a motor-powered sailboat pulled up to the dock on Alcatraz. A rich white woman from Sausalito was bringing food and water for the occupiers. She even brought a financial donation to help in getting other types of supplies. Boy, everyone was happy at the kindness and generosity of this lady.

"The next week, she was back with another load of supplies. The Indian men on the island lent a helping hand in unloading everything. After emptying the boat, they sat around the dock and got acquainted. It wasn't long afterward that the Indian women on the island began to suspect that something was wrong. We found out a little later that this white woman must have had fantasies about sleeping with Indian men.

"Next, she was bringing out alcohol and other drugs as well as supplies. We were trying to keep things clean on Alcatraz. Our 'friend' was not only violating our rules, but the damn bitch was sleeping with our men!

"The next time that beautiful sailboat pulled up to the dock, the white woman, now familiar with the place, jumped out onto the dock. She was wearing her tight white slacks again. The Indian women had seen her approaching, and many picked up sticks to be ready to meet her on the dock. Screaming obscenities, they started switching the woman with their sticks. She was surprised and held up her arms to fend them off as she retreated backwards in terror. Momentarily blinded by the attack, the woman fell off the dock into the freezing water of the bay. The Indian men, who up to this point had stood sheepishly watching, now went into action. They dragged the crying woman out of the water. She was hustled off to her boat, and we never saw her again."

There was also the story of the two preachers. Just two days after the joyous Thanksgiving celebration, E.E. Papke and his younger brother Ike were delivering supplies to the island. They were both huge Hawaiians who must have weighed close to 300 pounds each. After securing their boat, the *Sea Rogue*, the Papke brothers were starting to unload their cargo when they noticed a commotion near the drawbridge. Hustling on over, they found the island security forces, strong young Indian men, forming a line blocking the roadway to two white men.

"What's going on here?" E.E. asked the security men as he coolly surveyed the two whites.

"These guys say they're ministers, but it looks like they're just out here to make trouble for us," answered one of the security men.

"Do you gentlemen have any credentials or any proof that you are ministers?"

The younger of the two answered, rather arrogantly, "Our Bibles are our credentials and our mission here on Alcatraz is to preach the gospel of the Lord to these heathens!"

E.E. almost blew his stack over this remark and started to approach the two.

"Don't touch them!" shouted the security men. "Don't touch 'em!" E.E. Papke stopped and looked at the security men.

"They just want us to rough them up so they can complain to the authorities. They are nothing but bigots with Bibles and their only purpose in being here is to make trouble for us."

The Hawaiian turned back to the two Bible-toting would-be preachers and said slowly and with sincerity, "If you are true Christian people you will leave this island and these people alone."

Now, E.E. Papke was a guard at San Quentin prison. When there was a shakedown and the guards searching the prisoners' quarters encountered a prisoner who wouldn't leave his cell, they called for Papke. He would enter the cell, half swaggering and half waddling because of his immense size, and very calmly expel the reluctant prisoner. Two would-be troublemakers on Alcatraz would pose little threat to this man.

"We have the right to be here, and we are not leaving this island until we have the opportunity to preach the gospel to the heathens." The younger of the two had heard what the security man had said and was feeling confident. His threats were having the desired effect on the Indians. But he had not reckoned with the Papkes. The word "heathens" punched straight into E.E. like an ice pick.

"That's it fellas," he said calmly, moving forward. "We've tried to be nice to you and now we'll have to persuade you."

The younger man's confidence quickly evaporated as one burly hand grabbed him by the scruff of the neck and another grasped him by the seat of his britches, lifting him up until only his toes touched the ground.

"I think you have overstayed your welcome," said Papke as he walked the hapless zealot back to his boat. The older "preacher" followed meekly; he wasn't about to challenge the Papke brothers.

As the two frightened men got their boat underway, Papke called to them, "If you guys want to complain to the authorities about your treatment here, tell them it wasn't an Indian that threw you off the island, it was two Hawaiians!"

THANKSGIVING

Only a few days after the blockade ended a very special event took place on the island—Thanksgiving. Indians have traditionally enjoyed feast days, especially harvest days when we share the fruits of our labors, as we did with the Pilgrims. This Thanksgiving Day was special, since we shared not only the food but also all the tears, frustrations, and joys of the past weeks. Our harvest was the island, which we shared with all of our people.

Many Indians and Indian organizations helped plan the event. At the United Council, we discussed how to prepare the feast with the limited facilities on the island and decided to prepare the food in advance and haul it over as a sort of potluck. But before we began to prepare, Bratskellers Restaurant in Ghirardelli Square announced they would furnish all the fixings for the feast.

What a delicious turnabout of history! For the first Thanksgiving the Indians had not only taught the newly-arrived Pilgrims how to grow the food, but they had also brought most of the native foods to the feast— turkey, yams, cranberries, beans, squash, pumpkins, and deer. Now the Indians had landed on "white man's land" and the white man was going to provide the feast.

On November 27, Thanksgiving Day, Indians lined up to be ferried to the island. The blockade was over, so the bay was full of holiday boaters happy to take Indians over to Alcatraz. Many more boats full of festive spectators circled the island, enjoying this exciting and historic event.

Bobbie and I and our three teenage children stood in line with the other Indians. It was a colorful group of people; some wore gaily patterned Pendletons or long vivid dresses under their heavy coats. Many of the traditional dancers were already partially dressed in their regalia and carrying their feathered bustles. The lead singers, whistling some of the tunes they would sing later on the island, held their large war drums wrapped in their protective covers. The children ran around screaming, expressing openly the excitement we all felt inside.

"What if I get seasick?"

"Are the boats safe?"

"Are there sharks in the water?" Many questions made their way down the line. Bobbie had been raised in the Nevada desert and had little experience with boats on the ocean, and many others were in the same situation. But these concerns all added to the thrill of the event.

When our turn came, we boarded a tugboat with a good-natured captain. It wasn't the fanciest boat in the makeshift armada, but it was trustworthy. The captain invited the women into the protective warmth of the wheelhouse, and the men stood outside huddled together against the sea spray and brisk wind.

As we approached the island, it felt as if someone had turned up the dial on our excitement; this was the first visit to Alcatraz for most of us. The tugboat tied up alongside the barge at the dock, and island security greeted everyone with a smile and a joyous "Welcome to Alcatraz! You are now on Indian Land."

The security people helped the elderly visitors off the tugboat onto the gently rolling barge, and then escorted them down the wooden catwalk to the safety of the island. Our supplies were eagerly unloaded, and the smells of home-cooked stews and many Indian delights whet everyone's appetite. As soon as one boat was unloaded, it pulled away and another tied up and unloaded more Indians, many of whom felt relief at reaching land and the festivities.

I was visiting with some security people I knew—Al Miller, Joe Bill, and Charles Dana—when I spotted Alice Carnes coming off a boat with a couple of her daughters. I knew Alice because she was a valued member of the Ladies Club affiliated with the United Council. Few people realized that this was an especially moving day for this kind, gentle Choctaw woman from the hills of eastern Oklahoma. I had attended Haskell Institute with her son Ben, and it was there I learned of his older brother Clarence. In 1945 Clarence was sentenced to life imprisonment in Alcatraz for kidnapping. Clarence, known as the Choctaw Kid, was only 18—the youngest inmate in Alcatraz history. A year later, in May of 1946, he became one of the ringleaders in the bloodiest uprising in the prison's history. He was sentenced to die then, but his sentence was commuted and he later died as a free man.

I had no idea what was going through Alice's mind as she walked up the narrow catwalk to the island, smiling sweetly to those helping her, but it must have been an incredible experience for her to see a place of such horror transformed into a symbol of Indian pride.

By the time the boat from Bratskellers arrived, between 400 and 700 Indians had gathered on Alcatraz, many with food from home. Everyone assembled in the main recreation yard of the prison, surrounded by the high walls, topped with rusty barbed wire, that blocked our view of the bay. We were Indians surrounded by the old crumbling walls of oppression, and we were celebrating a new day.

A few years before, my Aunt Anna had given me my great-uncle's ceremonial pipe, and I brought it out on this historic day. In the recreation yard we set up a ceremonial altar where I lovingly filled the pipe. Richard Oakes, Cy Williams, John Folster, George Woodard and I prayed over the pipe for spiritual blessings for all the people sharing that special day on the island. This was a special moment for Indians. The Indian religions are not protected by the U.S. Constitution. Many Indians are imprisoned every year for practicing their beliefs, as I was fifteen years later. But on this day we prayed without fear, for we were on Indian land.

It was a beautiful and meaningful moment when the pipe passed among so many different Indian people. We were people from all four directions; our tribes came from the north and the south, the east and the west coasts. There was a hushed awe and respect among the crowd, for it is our tradition that as the pipe is passed one must be of good heart, mind, and body. One must release all negative thoughts such as anger or hate, or those thoughts will come back on oneself. I watched as young and old smoked. The island warriors, to whom we owed so much for physically risking themselves in the fight to take and hold the island, smoked and passed the pipe to those who were supporting their effort from the mainland. It was truly a united effort and we were truly Indians of All Tribes.

Bratskellers set up long tables with paper plates, cups, plastic utensils, and a truly sumptuous feast with all the trimmings. We added our home-cooked food to the spread. The non-Indian Bratskeller crew working together with the Indians in the spirit of friendship made a very special scene, and it was all recorded by the news media as they moved around the room to film and talk with many of the participants.

When dinner was ready to be served, a rush of people formed an instant line. Courtesy to the elders was not forgotten, however, and they were escorted to the front of the line. I remember Elmer and Martha St. John, both respected Lakota elders and medicine people, smiling as they acknowledged the young people of Alcatraz continuing the tradition of respecting the elders.

With their plates loaded down with food, people scattered around the area finding places to sit. Some sat on the sparse grassy areas, while most sat on giant concrete steps next to the main cell block. Cy and Aggie Williams sat next to us on the steps and visited. The two groups of pow wow singers, the Mockingbird Singers and the Oklahoma Singers, began to set up in the middle of the yard; the loud beat of their beautiful handmade drums reverberated off the surrounding walls, sending the hungry sea gulls flying.

The beat of the drum is to the Indian the beat of the heart. The playing of the drum, the dancing of moccasined feet, and the singing of our songs in our native tongues reaffirm to us that we will survive. Considering everything that has happened to Indians over the last centuries, this affirmation is a good one.

The dancers finished putting on their costumes and were drawn into a circle by the irresistible beat of the drum. The sound of the bells they wore around their ankles and the voices of the singers soon joined in with the drums to create an ancient music that became a spiritual renewal for all of us on the newly reclaimed Indian island. As we watched, we all gave thanks in our own way to the Great Spirit who had given us the moment, the land, and our fellow Indians and non-Indians who helped make it all possible.

Sadly, as evening approached we all said our goodbyes, packed up, and lined up on the dock to return to the mainland. A motorized sailboat took us to its berth in the Berkeley Marina, and from there we caught a ride with an Indian family to our car in the parking lot at Fisherman's Wharf. Our children were asleep before we even got onto the road, exhausted from the day's excitement. It was truly a day of thanksgiving.

DAILY LIFE

Soon after the Thanksgiving Day of unity, factions began springing up among us, and after that I rarely visited Alcatraz. Occasionally I brought out a celebrity or made the trip for a special meeting. I did not know what daily life on the island was like, except from secondhand reports from friends, the news, or my children. I do know that the early days of the occupation were like a honeymoon. All our dreams were becoming realities. The mainland support was at its height, the movement was still generally quite unified, and the excitement created an atmosphere of volunteerism and a real desire to make things work.

This was no easy task on an isolated, abandoned island. The island had been left to the elements from the time it was abandoned, so one major task was making the island habitable and hopefully even comfortable. Alcatraz was far from an island paradise, and the winter of 1969 was a cold, rainy season. The electrical systems in many of the buildings had been disconnected soon after the prison closed. To supplement the electrical power, the first of several generators was brought to the island. Safety was also a concern, especially with so many children running loose and elders visiting the island. One major project involved cleaning the treacherous tangle of vines and weeds that had overgrown the steep walkway.

Another problem was the plumbing; an Indian plumber found only three working toilets on the island when the occupation started. Within a few weeks he had 35 in working order. This was no simple task, as all useful plumbing equipment and materials had been stripped from the island after the prison was abandoned. Several old toilets had to be "cannibalized" for the parts to make one functional toilet. One can imagine the gratitude heaped on this plumber by island inhabitants; he fairly glowed with pride in his accomplishment. I guess that one could say he was flushed with success.

One of the great achievements of the occupation was the "Big Rock School" that opened to twelve students on December 11, 1969. An Indian education program run by Indians had been a long-standing dream. Significantly, it finally happened in the very prison where about 19 Hopi men were imprisoned for trying to keep their children at home instead of sending them away to Indian boarding schools. The U.S. Army came in with Navajo mercenaries and took the children, as well as any man who refused to give them up. The men were taken to the dungeons of Alcatraz as an example.

The Indian schools taught Indians nothing about their own heritage. From the late 1800s through the middle 1900s, repression of Indian culture was an enforced policy in Indian schools. In those days, Indian education consisted of programs to "civilize" the Indians with heavy doses of the white man's religion. Native languages were strictly forbidden. The missionaries in the mission school system justified this restriction by telling the children, "Indian language is the language of the heathen!"

The term "child abuse" was unknown, but the poor little "heathens" who violated the rules were punished in many abusive ways. A common punishment involved forcing a child to kneel for prolonged periods of time. A Navajo lady once told me that as a child in Indian schools she was forced to kneel next to the stove, holding aloft a chunk of firewood. After 30 minutes her little arms went numb with pain, but she wouldn't cry, as that would be giving in to her tormentors.

Another Indian lady told me that the punishment in her boarding school for speaking a native language was being forced to strip naked and stand in the hallway bent over for one hour. Joe Crown, one of my classmates at the Pipestone Indian Boarding School in Minnesota, could not speak English when he was first hauled off to school. This inability infuriated one of the nuns, who thought little Joe was just being stubborn. At first she locked him in a dark closet, thinking that somehow this would teach him the English language. After that experience, Joe did not dare to say anything. Daily prayer sessions taught him a few words, and he learned to respond to the greetings of the nuns and priests with a simple "Amen." Unfortunately, a nun once caught Joe speaking Chippewa to a classmate. The angry woman dragged Joe outside to the root cellar. Joe knew what she was going to do to him and fought back as best he could, but a five-year-old boy is no match for a full-grown woman. She forced the terrified child down the steps into the pitch-black cellar. Screaming and crying, Joe held up his little hands to stop the heavy door from swinging shut on him, but it caught the tips of three of his fingers and crushed them into a flat, bloody mess.

In contrast, traditional Indian people did not believe in beating or spanking their children in punishment; they considered anyone who would do so savage and barbaric. Many Indian people still carry scars from their early educational experiences. Fortunately, the schools had become a little more humane by the time I entered them, although in 1969 Senator Edward Kennedy issued a strong condemnation of the Indian educational system, calling it "A National Tragedy—A National Challenge."

American Indian scholars had long dreamed of a college or university with a strong native American Indian studies program in addition to all the conventional disciplines. The program would embrace all aspects of Indian life—history, language, spirituality, culture, arts, and more. This idea would be a radical departure from the educational programs that had been forced on the Indian people. Students would no longer suffer shame and humiliation for being themselves; Indian pride and integrity would start the long overdue rebuilding process.

Part of this dream came true on Alcatraz with the "Big Rock School." Instructors such as Linda Aranaydo (Creek), Vicky Santana (Blackfoot), Douglas Remington (Ute), and Woesha Cloud North (Winnebago), worked with aides such as Justine Moppin (Mono), Rosalie Willie (Paiute), and a number of teenagers to give each child as much individual and group attention as needed. They covered the usual subjects, but shifted the focus from just a purely white version of history to a perspective that included more native history and culture. Specific tribal information for each student was provided by the parents of the child and others familiar with the material.

The children of Alcatraz also received instruction in Indian cultural arts and crafts. Earl Livermore, the well-known Blackfoot artist from Montana who had been director of the San Francisco Indian Center, taught Indian art to anyone on the island who wanted to learn. Earl had been working on the Alcatraz proposal since the early days in the hope that he could set up an art school and crafts training center on Alcatraz. He was so committed to the idea that when the occupation became fact he resigned from the leadership of the Center and moved to Alcatraz to teach the young Indians on the island.

Earl also remained the coordinator for Indians of All Tribes Inc. and assisted in the administration of the many island art programs. Meade and Noreen Chibatti, Comanches from Oklahoma, gave dance and mu-

*Raymond Baird
(Sioux) shows
daughter Elaine, 5, the
fine points of feather
working. Photo
courtesy of the
Oakland Tribune.*

sic instruction. Meade was a nationally recognized Fancy Dancer who
had won the National Indian Fancy Dance competition in Anadarko,
Oklahoma in 1939. Francis Allen (Sac and Fox) taught native arts such
as beadwork, leatherwork, woodcarving, costume decoration, and sculp-
ture. A room adjacent to the old prison theater became a leathercraft
shop. A Tlingit from Alaska carved miniature totem poles, and many
others contributed to the artistic efforts of the Indians of All Tribes.

The Alcatraz Nursery School began in the office quarters of the main
cell block and then moved to the caretaker's building. The staff, which
included Maria Lavender (Yurok) and Lou Trudell (Sioux), started the
program as a day-care center for working mothers, but they soon turned
it into a preschool. The children played with clay and paint, heard Indian stories, and sang Indian songs.

An island health clinic had been started the day after the invasion,
and it was now run entirely by volunteers. Jenny Joe (Navajo), RN, and
Stella Leach (Colville-Sioux), LPN, kept it open daily; a mainland doctor, such as David Tepper, Robert Brennan, or Richard Fine, volun-
teered for a few hours each day.

The island kitchen was first set up in the main cell block, in the large
kitchen which was once used to prepare food for the convicts. Although

Cooking stew for dinner. Photo courtesy of the Oakland Tribune.

this location had the best facilities, it was too far from the old employee buildings where most of the Indians now lived. The kitchen was eventually moved down to the apartments to better serve the inhabitants. Butane stoves and food lockers cooled by dry ice or generators helped provide meals from the donated food and supplies. When the food donations weren't enough the Indians used the monetary donations to purchase more food supplies.

No home is complete without pets, and Alcatraz was no exception. One live turkey, two ducks, several rabbits, and two or three friendly dogs soon came to live on the island. Like young boys everywhere, the young Indian boys loved to fish, and there were several spots off the rocky Alcatraz shoreline which proved to be excellent fishing holes. Red snapper, bay perch, smelt, and occasionally striped bass provided many hours of exciting entertainment for the island youth, and good fresh fish were a welcome addition to any meal on the island.

With over 100 people living in a confined space, anything could and did happen. One woman left the island when the birth of her child became imminent; she gave birth to a normal and healthy child on the mainland. And on July 22, 1970, a little boy was born on Alcatraz to Lou and John Trudell. He weighed in at 7 pounds and was named Wavoka, after the legendary Paiute Messiah who originated the ghost dance back in the 1880s. The significance of the name was not lost to many Indians who knew of Wavoka's prophecy that the Indian and the buffalo would once again take their rightful place on the land. "Always do good, do no one harm" was the gentle Paiute's motto. He now has a namesake born on the Island of Hope, the island Alcatraz that symbolized a new beginning for the Indian.

Visitors streamed into Alcatraz almost constantly, especially in the early days. For many Indians, the trip to Alcatraz became almost a pilgrimage. After all, it was the only piece of land in the country "owned" by Indians of All Tribes, which meant that every Indian owned a piece of "the Rock." Any Indian was welcome on Alcatraz. If they chose to stay, after a week they were considered a resident and could participate in the governing of the island. This new Indian community attracted all kinds of Indians: college students, reservation Indians, "street people," mainland working people.

Many of the visitors and newcomers slept in the main cell block because of its notoriety, but they soon discovered that since the building's power plant had been dismantled, it was very cold and drafty. After one night visitors usually moved to more hospitable accommodations. Island residents chose living quarters in the three apartment houses, six cottages, two family duplexes, bachelors' quarters, or the chief medical officer's home. The warden's house was often used a guest house for the visiting non-Indians who were occasionally allowed to stay on the island.

Although I rarely went to Alcatraz and never stayed the night, two of my children, Julie and Adam, told me stories. Julie told of spending the night with her friends in one of the cells in the "D" block. The girls tied the cell door shut for protection, but when they woke the next day the cell door was untied and their camera was gone. Yet they were fed breakfast and given the run of the island. Julie remembers trying on clothes from the donation piles in the rummage room, while Adam recalls exploring the island and reveling in its notorious history. Julie says that although some "bad apples" went out to the island, most of the Indian occupants were good people.

A friend of ours, Justine, had planned on spending only one night on the island. The next day, the bay was too rough for her to leave and she had to spend another night. She became caught up in the spirit of the occupation and her "overnight stay" lasted for eighteen months. She told me she felt a special pride in that time.

"We were idealistic and believed that the occupation would finally call attention to Indian problems. There was a strong feeling of togetherness and unity and we all felt protected by the Great Spirit."

THE OCCUPATION OF ALCATRAZ

The island.

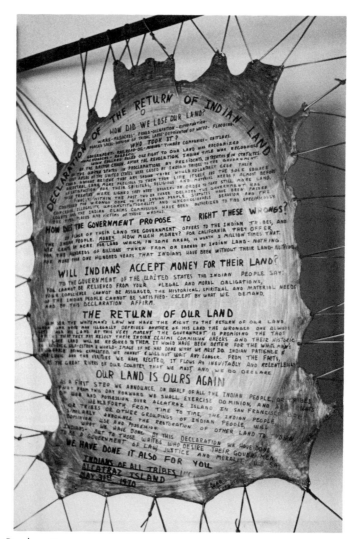

The Proclamation.

A prisoner's and an Indian occupier's view of the bay.

The lighthouse.

Indian occupier, a Paiute from Nevada.

The main cellblock.

Noreen and Meade Chibatti (Comanche).

Above: The fog moves into the courtyard.

Waiting for the boat.

Above: At the dock.

"First time away from the Navajo Reservation."

Above: Gino.

Occupiers.

Occupier in island truck.

Above: Michael Leach (Colville-Sioux).

Belva Cottier and a young friend.

Above: Waiting for the boat.

"Running into the sunshine." William Lopez (Pit River/Pomo) and playmate.

The water birds.

RICHARD OAKES

When people talk about Alcatraz, the one person they always mention is Richard Oakes. Even though he was involved for only a short time, no one else was so strongly identified with the occupation. Richard was young, articulate, ruggedly handsome, and passionately committed to the Indian cause. The media loved him.

Alcatraz changed many lives. It was a turning point, both good and bad, which shook many people out of one existence and into another. To some it brought struggle and divorce; to others it brought new pride and new friends. Alcatraz took Richard Oakes, an unknown student leader, and threw him into the center of a world-changing event. I remember him when we first met, and I remember how he changed with the circumstances. If there was a tragic character in the whole Alcatraz story, it would have to be Richard.

In traditional Indian cultures, younger men were not given leadership roles. Such positions were reserved for elders. An Indian with Richard's charisma, intelligence, and strong idealism would have been guided by the elders and trained to be a leader. After years of guidance and years spent gaining the wisdom that comes with age, he would have taken a role of leadership. But the luxury of tradition was not available to urban Indians, and perhaps this lack became Richard's undoing.

A Mohawk Indian born in 1942, Richard grew up on the St. Regis reservation near the Canadian border in New York. Reservation life had little to offer him, and when he was sixteen he went into the iron work for which his father and uncle had trained him. He worked all over New

Richard Oakes (left), meets with Cecil Poole (right), U.S. Attorney. John Hart,
(second from left), Alcatraz caretaker, and Dennis Turner, (second from right),
Luiseño Indian and member of Alcatraz Council, look on. Photo courtesy of
Associated Press.

England for eleven years until one day he decided to go to California.
After arriving, he drove a truck for a while and then became a bartender
in Warren's Bar, an "Indian" bar in the Mission District of San Francisco.

Richard eventually met and married Ann, a Pomo Indian raised on
the Stewart's Point Rancheria in Northern California. She already had
five children, who Richard accepted as his own. Ann was as shy and
withdrawn as Richard was bold and outgoing; she was never comfortable with all the publicity Richard brought upon them. She was looking
for a quiet, secure life as much as Richard was seeking to make his mark
in the world.

In the spring of 1969, 27-year-old Richard enrolled in the newly-
formed Native American Studies Program at San Francisco State University, along with many other Indians. It was there he became an activist, and a very prominent one: the visible symbol of the cause, the media
front. His brash style caused problems with the other Indian students,
but his behavior was appropriate to those radical times. His boldness
challenged the school administration and excited the news media, and

thus drew attention to Indian concerns. His passion for the Indian cause allowed him to do what many Indians with more withdrawn personalities found painful.

It was in October of 1969 that I met Richard Oakes at the media party in Sausalito and discussed the occupation with him. It was at that party that I got the first inklings of some of the problems we eventually had with Richard. Alcohol makes many oppressed people more belligerent and vocal around those they consider their oppressors; Richard unfortunately had this tendency. He had just agreed to become part of the leadership for the Alcatraz invasion, but the more he drank the louder and more belligerent he became. The last thing we wanted was to alienate the news media, so we hustled him out of the party.

In the earlier days, the news media considered Richard Oakes the leader and chief spokesman of the occupying forces. He was their personality, their hero. And why not? Richard was very handsome, with features so regular that one of the news stories compared him to a movie star. He commanded a great physical presence which the media immediately responded to. All of the attention was very intoxicating for Richard, as it would have been for anyone. As president of the Indian student group at San Francisco State, he was used to lots of attention from students and administrators. But that had all been relatively small potatoes compared to being thrust onto a stage with network television cameras and reporters from all over the world.

Early in the occupation, Earl Livermore and I attended a press conference in San Francisco. As I walked into the room my eyes were drawn to a big notice posted on the wall facing me proclaiming, "Indians on Alcatraz will rule Alcatraz." We saw this as the beginning of a power play and a serious split between the people on the island and the people on the mainland. The press conference began, and Richard and his people came in and sat down at the table. Earl and I stood watching from the side; Richard made no move to include us in the proceedings. Tim Findley came over and commented, "Well, Adam, Earl, it looks like it's all over for you guys."

"Yep," we said, and smiled back. It was a hard pill to swallow.

Three weeks later, in an interview with Lynn Ludlow of the *San Francisco Examiner*, Richard proudly proclaimed, "It's the first time we've gotten all the Indians together—perhaps we can develop an all-tribes consciousness." The headline read: "Oakes Has One Goal for Alcatraz: Unity." For those of us now excluded from leadership, there was great irony in that word "unity."

Yet, the generation gap was a part of many student and radical groups of the 1960s. It was common to resent the older generation and lump people with jobs and houses into the category of the "overly cautious" middle class. Moderation and willingness to negotiate were not popular qualities in those fiery years. And I have to admit, I had my prejudices against the "overly bold" students and radicals. Divisiveness, whether between neighboring tribes or generations, is an old story to Indian people; it has plagued many past attempts at Indian unity. And we later realized that conflict was exactly what the government had anticipated.

While the "unified" *Examiner* interview still sat on the newsstands a disgruntled group on Alcatraz began plotting Richard's removal. Some claimed Richard was "too self-centered and arrogant"; others claimed he was "trying to run the whole show." A few weeks later there was a power conflict between Richard's supporters and another group.

While this struggle was going on, tragedy struck the island. On January 5, 1970, Richard's 13-year-old adopted daughter Yvonne fell down three flights of stairs in the officers' quarters. She was rushed to a hospital on the mainland but soon died.

The death shocked the island residents. The invincibility they had all felt was deeply shaken, and drastic changes began. Just a few months before, Richard had concluded the Ludlow interview with the words, "We've got the ultimate punishment for any Indian on our island—we ask them to leave." The Indians who took over Alcatraz asked Richard to leave.

This didn't stop him. In June, he was arrested on trespassing charges while supporting the Pit River Indian effort to "reclaim" a huge parcel of land near Mount Shasta. His passion for the Indian cause was as strong as ever. A short time later, Richard was back in San Francisco drumming up support for the Pit River Indians. While relaxing in Warren's Bar where he once worked as a bartender, Richard got into an argument with a young Samoan. The argument turned into a fight, and the young Samoan smashed a pool cue over Richard's head.

He was in a coma for a long time after that beating and many gave him up for dead. Richard's condition turned around when the Iroquois medicine man and activist, Mad Bear, and another medicine man went to Richard's room and worked on him. Richard came out of the coma, but he remained partially paralyzed in a wheelchair.

Against his doctor's advice, Richard later checked out of the U.C. Medical Center where he was undergoing therapy. Two weeks later he and his family were about to start off on another project. They were going to travel across America in an old battered bus, Richard's "traveling college," visiting Indian reservations and settlements. Richard wanted to record and document what he learned and bring it back to teach a "real American history." He hoped to return with not just one bus, but "with a caravan—an army—of Indian people to reclaim their history and their land with new pride." Whether he meant this to happen on Alcatraz, I didn't know. In any case, Richard's condition kept the "traveling college" at home.

I saw Richard later at an anti-Vietnam War demonstration; I was at the microphone when he was wheeled out to speak to the crowd. Seeing him in that chair really affected me. He had such physical presence and showed such potential of being a a valuable and lasting leader. Now he was not only deposed from his leadership position, but also partially paralyzed and dependent on others for help to move.

It was some time before he was out of that wheelchair, and he still wasn't quite fit when he went up to Mendocino County and got involved in an incident that cost him his life. As the story goes, a few Indian boys were riding horses that belonged to a nearby YMCA camp. Security officers from the camp confronted the boys, and an argument began. Richard was there and tried to intervene to calm things down. The argument ended, but the fact that Richard had taken the boys' side didn't sit too well with the security officers. The same conflict came up again, and another argument began. The security officers claimed that Richard made a motion toward his jacket pocket, as if reaching for a weapon. With no hesitation, one of the officers pulled out his 9mm automatic and shot Richard right through the chest. The shot killed him.

Richard had no weapon. The officer had met Richard before, and should have realized that he limped and was in a weakened condition. Even if he had been armed, Richard was incapable of putting up much of a fight. There was a trial and the officer was found not guilty. The Bay Area community, both Indians and non-Indians, felt the loss deeply, and Richard Oakes was greatly missed.

OUR CONFLICTS

From the beginning, we wanted Alcatraz to be a showcase of Indian virtues and Indian greatness. It would display to the world the most magnificent achievements of our people: our courage; our sense of poetry, oratory, and art; our love of the land; our devotion to family; our contributions to the institutions and economies of the world; our laughter; our deeply felt and deeply experienced spiritual ways. In many regards, Alcatraz was such a place, and again and again I return to those memories to refresh and renew my spirit. I'm sure many others do also.

But in other ways, Alcatraz also became a showcase for the problems that have plagued Indians throughout our recent history—most notably alcohol, drugs, and factionalism, a tragic tendency to fight among ourselves instead of uniting to fight a common enemy. It is hard to talk about these things, but they too are part of the story.

We had hoped to keep Alcatraz free of booze and drugs (as if any society in human history has ever done so). When I look back, this goal becomes even more preposterous in light of the time and the place: the drug-soaked culture of the late 1960s in let-it-all-hang-out San Francisco. Yet we did make the effort, and in the early months we succeeded. Perhaps part of what made the first Thanksgiving so uplifting and celebratory was its blessed lack of alcohol.

But many of our supporters were part of the San Francisco counterculture, for whom drug use was a routine part of life. For many Indians, alcohol abuse was a life-long habit. The influx of drugs and alcohol was inevitable, and by January of 1970 an occasional load of booze and drugs was making its way to the island. Some of the young warriors took to warming themselves on those long, cold winter nights by chug-a-lugging at the contraband bottles. Fighting began to break out occasionally.

At first, the security forces made an open show of pouring out the contraband bottles. But once it became tacitly acknowledged that alcohol was being used on the island, many became more bold. Bonfires were a common sight on the the the dock on cold winter nights. While the island security kept watchful eyes on the water for any potential moves by the federal authorities, men and women stood around the campfires singing songs, playing radios, laughing, telling stories, and eventually sneaking a bottle.

It is impossible for some Indians to drink in a socially casual way. Alcoholic beverages are still banned on most reservations; few people realize that the U.S. Government once banned serving or selling alcohol to Indians, a ban which remained in effect until 1952. Today, most reservations prefer to remain dry. Bootlegging on the reservations continues to be a profitable business, as it was across the nation during Prohibition. As a result of these constraints, many Indians developed an unhealthy drinking style called "chug-a-lugging." Cans of beer or bottles of strong liquor are passed around a group; everyone takes a swig until the alcohol is gone and the empty container is quickly thrown away to destroy the evidence. Just a few passes of the liquor and most of the group becomes totally drunk.

One evening on Alcatraz, a fight broke out between a couple of the men. Their powerful blows landed solidly with the the sound of thunder, and the commotion brought others hustling down to the dock to see what was going on.

"Hey, what the hell are they fighting for?" asked a newcomer.

"Unity!" replied the security man.

Although there were undoubtedly undercover agents on the island, there was no visible police force to uphold the laws of California, and the use of drugs and alcohol eventually became quite blatant. This aspect of Indian life shocked some members of the press as well as many of our supporters. There are many people who are enamored with Indians when we are spiritual, poetic, exploited, or standing up to the government for our rights. Many, however, have more trouble accepting some of the other parts of Indian life—the depression, the self-hatred, the alcoholism, the self-destruction, and the cynicism that come with generations of humiliation and defeat.

Reports began to appear in the press of alcohol and drug abuse as well as infighting among the island residents. Back at the United Council, we discussed the way Alcatraz was being depicted.

"What the heck is so bad about those things?" exclaimed Cy Williams. "Just look at any reservation in this country and see what goes on."

Fount Washburn, a light-skinned Cherokee whose speech verged on the accent of his native Oklahoma, cut in. "Ain't that like what we said in the proclamation? If people can get themselves upset about the living conditions for Indians on Alcatraz, why can't they get just as fired up about the living conditions on reservations where we're under direct government control?"

"Damned right!" answered Wilson Harrison, a Navajo with the rugged wind-carved countenance of his pure-blood family. "People seem to care more about what is going on at Alcatraz than they do about how tough and poor it always is on the reservations."

Some of us felt there was a decidedly beneficial side to all the negative publicity. Many of the reporters talked about how the alcohol abuse grew out of the depressed and hopeless conditions of the reservations and how they were often promoted by white society. While we were pained by the exposure, we comforted ourselves with the hope that now perhaps we could expect greater understanding of the Indians' plight and of the damage done by centuries of ruthless exploitation.

Others, however, particularly those who lived on the island and were the subjects of the articles, had a different point of view. They saw any media criticism as not only unwelcome, but a sign of betrayal. For example, Tim Findley wrote an article for the *San Francisco Chronicle* in which he mentioned the "three B's: the ageless trio of trouble among the red men—booze, boredom, and, most seriously, bickering." This comment was not well received. Despite the overwhelmingly positive coverage and direct help that Tim had given to Alcatraz, for a time he was told he was not allowed onto the island.

This animosity toward the media and hypersensitivity to criticism filled some of us with horror. We needed the media to tell the story of Alcatraz. They had been our greatest asset from the beginning, and we greatly feared any alienation. Yet the situation continued to deteriorate.

Island security began to try to "protect" the island from the media. The Bureau of Caucasian Affairs (BCA) was initially created as a mild and cynical jab at the Bureau of Indian Affairs (BIA). Their role was to control and regulate the activities of the five white caretakers on the island, but they soon began controlling all the white visitors. The BCA began wearing red arm bands and calling themselves "Security." The arm bands were soon replaced by special jackets with "Alcatraz Security" emblazoned on the back, and the BCA ranks swelled to include over 50 Indians. Despite the island ban on weapons, they conducted frequent training sessions to practice repulsing federal attempts to remove the Indians or retake the island.

But the government had its hands full. The controversial war in Southeast Asia had put the nation in deep distress, and the last thing the government wanted was a confrontation with Indians in the United States. So the feds had to be content to play a waiting game.

In retrospect, it seems odd that we tolerated a paramilitary force on the island with such equanimity. Our tolerance was partly due to the obvious fact that since we didn't have the protection of the city police, we needed some kind of security force. It was also partly due to the tone of the times. In the late 1960s and early 1970s, Americans on both the right and the left had grown to accept paramilitary organizations, from the Black Panthers to right-wing gun advocates. American radicals and liberals, previously peace-oriented and very anti-gun, now found themselves inviting the Black Panthers to speak at rallies, using the Hell's Angels as security police in the Rolling Stones concert at Altamont, and romanticizing groups such as the Weather Underground and the Symbionese Liberation Army. The revolutionary, whether George Washington or Eldridge Cleaver, was the hero of the times.

The security forces had many interesting adventures, including the famous arrow incident. During the time Alcatraz was used as a federal prison, buoys circled the island like a colorful necklace, marking a zone of two hundred yards which no boats were allowed to enter. The prison authorities didn't want any inmates to escape by boat; they took no chances. If a boat strayed too close, a bullet across the bow or a burst of machine-gun fire was enough to convince any skipper to push the throttle full open and beat a hasty retreat from the danger zone. Everyone remembered this intimidating policy long after the prison was abandoned.

But once the Indian occupation became an accomplished fact, tour boats loaded with gawking, camera-toting tourists moved in closer and closer. The island residents didn't appreciate being gawked at like animals in a zoo. They shouted at the boats to stay away and stop endangering the smaller supply boats tied up to the island wharf. It didn't do any good. The big tour boats kept coming closer to allow their patrons the best possible look at the wharf area and the old fortress looming over it.

The final straw came when a tour boat came too close and its wake slammed a small supply boat violently against the dock's pilings. The Indians were furious. In spite of the island's ban on weapons, one Indian had managed to smuggle a bow and arrow onto the island. He notched an arrow and let it fly toward the offending craft. That fragile little arrow broke on contact with the steel hull of the tour boat, but the tiny "clink" it made was heard all the way to the San Francisco federal office building. When the officials there were notified of the incident, they were outraged that the Indians had resorted to arrow-dynamics to repel intruders from the island.

The Alcatraz Indians held a news conference to respond to the criticism. John Trudell of the Alcatraz Council stated, "We asked the ferry people to stop this, we asked the Coast Guard to take action, and finally, we said we wanted it stopped. And yet it continued.

"With one 42-cent arrow, we stopped it."

But the young security people did not usually see such excitement, and they were not content with the waiting game the government was playing. They wanted the thrilling adrenaline rush that comes from confronting the threat of danger. Their new authority to maintain law and order on the island contrasted sharply with the way Indians were usually "bossed" around by others. This authority energized them—now it was their turn to be the boss and do the "bossing." Some say that as the BCA became more powerful the situation on the island began to resemble the nightmarish book by William Golding, *The Lord of the Flies*. Although it was probably an exaggeration, the comparison still made many of us uneasy, and the aggressive activities of the BCA eventually drove a wedge between those on Alcatraz and those of us who tried to support it from the outside.

You can imagine my feelings at this time. I had seen the positive impact and results of the Alcatraz occupation on the national level. And although the occupation was having problems, it was apparent that the longer it lasted, the more we could accomplish on the national level. Our next attempt to support Alcatraz became, unfortunately, a symbol of the growing tension. As public interest and support dropped off, the United Council started discussing ways to develop a self-sustaining economy for the island. A logical solution evolved—why not conduct tours of the old prison island? Guided tours, managed by the island Indians, would assure a steady income for the occupation. We knew, of course, that we had absolutely no control over what happened on Alcatraz, but we thought we'd give it a try anyway.

I contacted the manager of Harbor Tours with a proposal for a joint venture with the Indians of Alcatraz. There was no question in his mind about the economic possibilities for his company, as well as for the occupation. I told him that my role was simply to open discussion on the feasibility of such a proposal; I would have to get the approval of the Indians on the island.

Armed with this positive interest, I proceeded to Alcatraz to present the proposal. The public tours of the island would be in designated areas only: the fort, the main cell block, and the shop area. The employees' quarters, the area where the Indians lived, would be off-limits to the visiting public. But instead of discussing how such a proposal might have a positive economic effect, the island residents turned the idea down flat.

"We are not going to be like monkeys in a zoo," they protested. "We got the island, and we're going to hold onto it, on our terms!"

Which of us was right? At the time I felt angry and frustrated. I felt that we had lost a unique opportunity to raise much needed money and further educate the public. At the same time, I could understand their refusal to turn a revolution into a commercial activity or cater in any way to the dominant culture. Although I felt that this was very bad strategy, I could understand it, and I went on to support Alcatraz in other ways.

What I had not known at the time of this bitter dispute was the fact that our decisions were irrelevant. When the island council finally decided to conduct tours, the Coast Guard refused to give sanction to the ferries needed to bring the people to Alcatraz. As all our bickering over power widened the gap between us, the government really held the trump card. And they continued to wait and we continued to fight amongst ourselves.

THE MEDIA

Like any populist cause, the Alcatraz occupation relied on the media from the very beginning. Fighting the government and its vast bureaucracy and resources takes a lot of support, and this requires a channel to inform potential supporters. The media also act as watchdogs. The civil rights marches in Alabama would have ended in much more death and violence if the media had not been there to spread the word of what was happening. In the 1960s, especially after the Democratic Convention riots, the common phrase was "the whole world is watching." In the critical early months of Alcatraz it was very true.

Our plans always included the media, and they soon become an integral part of the occupation. Their most critical functions were protecting the effort from a harsh government reaction and creating the necessary public support. Tim Findley, who threw the media party where we announced the invasion, was probably the most dedicated of the media supporters. Most did not participate so directly, but their interest in effect validated and thus created the level of interest in Alcatraz.

The media support began the very moment the Indians landed on the island. Most Americans thought Indians all lived someplace in the Midwest, but suddenly a bunch of idealistic Indians landed on an island right in the middle of San Francisco Bay, risking everything to get their message heard. And this happened in the late 1960s, when the ethnic groups that had previously been portrayed as stupid, violent people were being portrayed in a much more favorable light, even if it was often a romanticized glow. Popular movies were showing Indians as intelligent, honorable people who had been the victims of massacres, rather than the ones fighting against the white man in the white hat. The U.S. military, bogged down in Vietnam committing atrocities seen daily on television newscasts, were no longer the heroes. The truth was coming out.

In the midst of this new attitude came Alcatraz. A group of un-armed, downtrodden Indians, women and children included, were pro-testing right in the middle of one of the biggest and most liberal met-ropolitan areas in the country, in full view of millions watching on television newscasts. What could the government do? If they sent armed soldiers to retake the island, the world would be watching. And if someone on the island was armed, there could be violence. If anyone was hurt or killed during a government takeover, the media would see it all and the government would be swamped with protests.

I knew all of this, and had been catering to the news people for some time as president of the United Council. I had seen the power of the media the year before when the Intertribal Friendship House provided food baskets for needy families at Christmas. In years past the generosity of the public had provided plenty of food, but in December of 1968 the campaign had only received four cases of cake topping.

I kept listings of every newspaper and wire service in the Bay Area, along with the name of an editor or writer I could call when I had a newsworthy story. After a few calls to contacts, the Friendship House was swarming with television crews and news reporters. They quickly produced a touching and appealing human interest Christmas story. The ladies at the Friendship House told of the lack of public response, and showed the almost empty pantry.

The public response was overwhelming. Carloads of needed supplies arrived at the Friendship House, and many others gave money. The extra food provided needed assistance for months to come, and I gained a new respect for the influence and power of the news media. I also learned that there are plenty of good-hearted people willing to give to a good cause if they are aware of it, an understanding which proved to be a valuable resource during the Alcatraz occupation.

Indeed, there was a growing international awareness of the plight of the American Indian. Edward Kennedy had even prepared a report with documented proof that the federal government had failed to help the Indian people. Alcatraz voiced these concerns, and to our surprise many people were favorably impressed by what they saw, heard, and read. Thanks to Alcatraz, the media was eager and willing to tell our story.

Unfortunately, the hostility felt by some island residents blinded them to the fact that the news media was our greatest ally. When reporters covered some of the problems on Alcatraz, the island council was quick to condemn them. Thomas Hannon, regional administrator of the General Services Administration, commented in an interview with Kitty Archibald of the Bay Area Publishing Company:

> *Reporters are not allowed on Alcatraz unless the Indians can be guaranteed that they will write a "favorable" story. As an example, just last week a reporter for one Bay Area newspaper called the shots as he saw them from personal observations out there, and he has now been barred from the island. Numerous other reporters have lost their re-entry to the island because of unfavorable stories.*

International journalists were stymied by the permit system used by the council on Alcatraz. "Our press credentials are accepted all over the world, but they are not good enough to get us out to that little island!" complained a reporter from Germany.

The media backlash was predictable. The Alcatraz Indians took the short view of the issue and chose to look out for their own interests, an attitude which further eroded the relationship with the mainland groups. The press picked up the unresponsive attitude and passed it on to the public. In reaction, the public's formerly generous donations to Alcatraz diminished, and their support did as well.

Yet the occupation contributed to the public interest in other Indian issues and concerns around the country. Al Silbowitz, manager of KPFA radio in Berkeley, set up more than 500 pounds of antennas, transmitters and microphones on the island. The employees of the "listener owned" station covered the cost of over $2000, thus putting "Radio Free Alcatraz" on the air. Daily live broadcasts produced by the Indians covered a broad span of topics: Native American culture, current Indian affairs, and Indian history. John Trudell, a Santee Sioux, was the main announcer.

Al Silbowitz commented to the press, "We're just offering them the outlet. We don't want to crowd them and we're not telling them what to do. We want it to be their own thing."

More glamorous support for the occupation came from the famous. There were concerts by Buffy St. Marie and other singers and groups who came to entertain the liberating Indian forces. Movie stars came to visit the island, including Anthony Quinn, who played Zorba the Greek; the singer Ed Ames stayed for a whole day. One day at the United Council I even got a call from the Merv Griffin show. I gave them some background on Alcatraz, and Merv and his entire crew went out to the island and filmed all day. Merv Griffin gave a hell of a presentation on network television.

GOVERNMENT REACTION

During the nineteen months of the Indian occupation, radical and anti-government activities were taking place all over the nation. Black Power, Yellow Power, Red Power, Student Power, Women's Lib, sexual freedom, environmentalism, free-speech, the anti-war movement...you name it, it was happening. So was the conservative backlash—Nixon was president, Reagan was governor of California, the middle class was trying to hold on to their outdated values and their kids. Then came Alcatraz.

The relationship between the government and the Indian occupiers was a product of the times. The government would probably have been glad to hand Alcatraz over to the Indians, but conservative voters would have called that giving in to the "radicals." Such an action would also have encouraged other groups to reclaim other lands. The government needed to save face in the situation; the problem was that the Indians did also. As one reporter wrote, "The Indian occupation of Alcatraz was like a big white elephant hanging around the neck of the government." And the whole world was watching.

The Justice Department summoned Commissioner of Indian Affairs Robert Bennett and asked if the Indians were breaking any federal laws in their takeover of Alcatraz. He replied that he didn't think so, but added that they should wait and see. This was their only alternative. Storming Alcatraz with American troops might end up in another Indian massacre, which would have been the worst possible outcome for the government in those days of increasingly violent protests against U.S. involvement in Southeast Asia.

The first thing the government did try was the blockade. It was a non-violent action that should have worked, except every would-be pirate with a boat on the bay wanted to run the blockade. The blockade failed. Unfortunately, all initial negotiations with the government also failed. The government's only position was "leave the island and then we can negotiate." To the Indians, this idea sounded too much like the promises of the last century: "Move onto the reservation and we will take care of you." The Alcatraz Indians were not having any of it.

The government people then decided that they needed to talk to a "more representative body of Indians in the Bay Area." They put up a $50,000 grant to establish the Bay Area Native American Council (BANAC). Federal officials hinted that the new organization would be able to submit funding proposals for programs that would work on a much broader scale than the existing ones.

All the Bay Area Indian groups got together, and after a series of hasty meetings we agreed in principle to the umbrella organization. Representatives from the Indians of All Tribes of Alcatraz knew of the government's intentions and turned out in force for the meetings. They insisted on having veto power over any negotiations or actions proposed by BANAC regarding Alcatraz. I strongly opposed this power, as it would render the entire Bay Area Indian population helpless before the small group holding Alcatraz. Wasn't Alcatraz supposed to represent Indians of all tribes?

The Alcatraz occupants asserted, "We put our lives on the line to take that island and you guys sit in the safety of your homes. We are not going to be sold out to the government by you!" Their viewpoint was understandable, but many of us who had been working with and fighting the government for a number of years saw it as very short-sighted.

BANAC accepted the veto power by Indians of All Tribes of Alcatraz. But once BANAC lost its representative nature, the government lost interest in negotiations. House Resolution 1042, which proposed turning the title of Alcatraz over to Indian control, died a silent death. We had been given a fantastic opportunity to join forces with all the tribal groups and collectively negotiate for the establishment of any number of meaningful and worthwhile programs around the Bay Area. When I consider what we might have achieved for Bay Area Indians, I feel very sad. But on the other hand, it could have been just another government trick.

The next government action against Alcatraz began in January when Washington announced that the title to the island would be transferred from the General Services Administration (GSA) to the Department of the Interior for the purpose of converting the prison site into a national park which would be the centerpiece in the Golden Gate Recreation Area. The announcement came from Interior Secretary Walter Hickel, and the San Francisco papers quoted him as saying the Alcatraz project would "particularly emphasize the contribution of the American Indian to the nation." Robert Robertson, executive director of the National Council for Indian Opportunity, followed through with a proposal for an Indian Museum and a cultural center on Alcatraz. He also proposed that Indians be trained as park rangers to conduct tours on the island. Details of the master plan for the new national park were to be worked out with Indian representatives.

Representatives of the Alcatraz Indians turned the plan down flat. A local paper reported they were "determined to settle for nothing less than getting title to the island and seeing its conversion into an Indian university and cultural center."

In an interesting aside, Thomas Hannon, regional head of the GSA, announced to the media that transferring the title to the Interior Department would take several weeks and sometime afterwards a government contractor would begin demolishing the crumbling prison buildings. In the meantime, Hannon stated, there would be no government interference with the Indian occupiers, nor would any legal action be taken if any of the old furniture or other property, a few inoperative vehicles and one working truck, turned up missing. As it turned out, not all the government agencies kept the latter promise.

The government next approached the Alcatraz situation by trying to make a secret deal through *San Francisco Chronicle* reporter Tim Findley. Thomas Hannon called Tim to his home in Tiburon and made a proposal to trade Alcatraz for a part of Fort Mason. This was an incredible offer. Fort Mason, located at the foot of Russian Hill next to Fisherman's Wharf, was one of the prime pieces of property in San Francisco. Its old military buildings were in good shape and its convenient location would eliminate the problem of boat transportation across the Bay. This was the deal of a lifetime for Bay Area Indians. Tim relayed this information to me and the Indians of All Tribes on Alcatraz. After a short debate, the proposal was turned down, over my vocal and written objections. You can imagine the frustration the government and I felt after losing what would have been a "sweetheart" deal for the Indians. But since it was not pursued, I will never know if the Fort Mason idea was a real proposal or just another government trick.

There were other "deals," such as the one proposed by Robert Robertson. He stated that if the Indians left, the government would hire five Indians as caretakers. The Indians replied that if they could pay five Indians, they could pay 100 Indians. The government didn't reply.

About six months later, as patience was wearing thin, the government again adopted an attitude of "No More Mister Niceguy" and started tightening down the screws: if the Indians lived without electricity and water on the reservations back home, they could do without them on Alcatraz. Early in the morning of May 9, 1970, a Coast Guard cutter pulled alongside the Alcatraz dock, hooked up the only water barge on the West Coast, and towed it away from the island. The message to the occupants of Alcatraz was "we are only going to do some repairs." The barge was never seen again. About the same time, the General Services Administration withdrew the last of its caretakers from the island with the announcement that the government would no longer supply fresh water to the island.

The water barge had supplied the island by making regular trips to the mainland to fill up its tank with 250,000 gallons of water. The barge then returned to the island and pumped its precious cargo into the water tower. That homely black hunk of iron was the life line for Alcatraz. Unfortunately, the government didn't really repair it; instead they sold it as scrap metal. The lack of running water caused some problems for the Indians, but ironically this lack has also come back to haunt the government. It has been more than eighteen years since Alcatraz became a park, and for all of that time the National Park Service has been hauling water to the island in puny five-gallon plastic containers. The island staff and the one million people that visit Alcatraz each year all use the same water. So next time you are on Alcatraz and you have to use one of those smelly portable toilets, thank your government.

Next the federal government pulled the electrical power to the island. The electricity ran the lighthouse and the foghorn, and the Indians had tapped into it to run their electrical system. When queried, an official responded, "The Indians are blowing too many fuses with their 150-watt bulbs." The Coast Guard dispatched maintenance personnel to the island, supposedly to repair the reserve generators. Instead of making needed repairs, the repair workers took vital parts, rendering the generators inoperative.

The government's next move was to place buoy lights around Alcatraz to warn ships away from the island. These two changes greatly disturbed the San Francisco Board of Supervisors. The lighthouse and foghorn on Alcatraz were signatures of the San Francisco Bay, and things were not the same without them. The little buoys had foghorns on them, but they couldn't match the timbre of the mighty blasts of the horn on the lighthouse beacon. Even the shipping industry was upset with the government; they felt the buoys provided insufficient protection for their ships compared to the lighthouse and foghorn on Alcatraz.

Despite protests, the government thought they had won that round in their battle to evict the stubborn occupiers of Alcatraz. They had not, however, realized the "injunuity" of the Indians. Tapping their network of mainland support, the Alcatraz Indians obtained a generator and hooked it up to the lighthouse. They then called a press conference at Fisherman's Wharf.

"The light is needed by the ships at sea, and by the eyes on land which watch over them and guide them," announced John Trudell. "For us on the island and for Indians everywhere, it is a symbol of the re-kindled hope that some day the just claims and rightful dignity of the American Indians will be recognized by our fellow citizens. It was in peaceful search of this recognition that we came to the island last November. As long as the light glows, the search will go on."

Trudell's eloquence and easy confidence showed that at last a single leader had emerged who was accepted as both spokesperson and strat-egist for Alcatraz. Trudell was a young man in his 20s with a long flow of brown hair and a light complexion that did not show much of his Sioux blood. Trudell's quiet, studied approach to the problems and conflicts on the island seemed to win the trust of the other occupiers, although he was largely unknown to the mainland group. But there could be no denying the firm intelligence and polished resolve with which he handled himself.

That night the mighty glow of the searchlight cast its brilliant arc across the bay and the great foghorn roared its approval. All the people of the Bay Area rejoiced with the Indians—the light was on again! The federal bureaucrats must have bit their lips over that one, for they real-ized the Indians had won a major public relations battle.

The Indians on the island were feeling pretty good at this point. For just a bunch of "redskins" they had managed to outfox the government on a number of counts. And despite all the problems confronting them, one basic fact was an accepted reality—the Indians held the island. The Indians of Alcatraz basked in the glow of the restored lighthouse beacon and the renewed public support.

Two weeks later the most sensational and controversial event of the entire occupation hit the island. On the evening of June 1, 1970, a di-sastrous fire caused more damage than the prison riot of 1946.

"Fire! Fire!" shouted an Indian man as he ran into the mess hall sometime after 10 p.m. Several people were doing craftwork, others were sleeping. They all sprang up at his words. Sheer terror struck many who believed it was the long-expected counterattack by the government.

Outside, bright flames were shooting out of the windows of the warden's house. It was useless to try the faucets; the water barge had been hauled away three weeks earlier and there was no reserve supply in the water tower. The Indians quietly organized a makeshift water-bucket brigade, but they soon discovered the old recreation building was also ablaze. The dry wood-frame structure burned with such intensity that the blistering heat made the roadway by the building impassable; the steep and dangerous steps past the old fort were the only way down to the water. The few buckets of water that did reach the fire were no match for the blazing inferno. All the people of Alcatraz could do was sit and watch the fearsome fire consume virtually all it touched.

Many tribes consider fire to be a sacred object—something to be handled with reverence and respect. An offering of tobacco or cedar, along with a prayer, is given to the sacred fire after entering the tribal longhouse. The fire used to heat the stones in the sweat lodge ceremonies is considered sacred, and it is acknowledged in the ceremony with reverence. In 1836 the Cherokee people carried their sacred fire all the way from Georgia to Tallequah, Oklahoma, where it still burns to this very day, protected and cared for in the traditional ways.

Now the fires of Alcatraz glowed like spirits gone mad through the dense night fog above San Francisco Bay. No longer the warm and protective light that lived comfortably within lodges, the fire had become an awesome power that would strike down anyone who dared challenge its might. The great beacon in the lighthouse, badly damaged by the heat, stopped flashing its precious light. The voice of the mighty foghorn was once again stilled.

"The light is out. The light is dead," remarked one Indian who remembered John Trudell's statement that as long as the light glowed the search for recognition would go on. Looking at that fire-blackened lighthouse, the struggle seemed to be all over.

Reporters trooped to Alcatraz the next day. The burned shells of the warden's house and the infirmary were hopeless cases; the recreation hall was nothing but ashes. But once again, the maverick nature that seems to come with living in the Bay Area came to the rescue. *San Francisco Chronicle* Editor Scott Newhall was a maverick among mavericks and an unabashed romantic whose high-rise apartment overlooked the bay and the sweeping light of Alcatraz. Newhall had always found the light soothing. When he heard the report of the damage to the lighthouse, Newhall assigned his chief engineer the unusual task of finding a replacement bulb, new wiring, and generator parts to restore what he considered an essential element of the San Francisco character and his personal view.

A team of *Chronicle* people, including reporter Tim Findley, traveled to Alcatraz with electrical wire, replacement parts, and a new bulb.

After several hours of sweaty effort, the generator started with a roar, the breaker switch was thrown, and the light sprang to life once again. Smoke-blackened faces broke into wide smiles and the Indians broke into enthusiastic applause. "As long as the light glows, there is hope!"

Immediately after the smoke cleared on the island, government representatives began claiming that the Indians had deliberately set the fires. The Indians accused the government of sending saboteurs to the island. They claimed that two men who must have slipped through island security patrols had been spotted running from the fires just after they began.

Picture it. A government official and an Indian standing face to face, pointing at each other, yelling, "He did it!"

There was no hard evidence found to support either charge, but it seemed that the news media slightly favored the government's opinion. This preference may have been due in part to the unfavorable treatment the media received from the island security concerning their press passes to the island.

Yet despite all the catastrophes, the Indians were still holding steadfastly to the island a year after the occupation began. Three of the original fourteen that landed on the night of November 20 were still living on the island: LeNada Means, John White Fox, and Jim Vaugh. The government's war of attrition had become a waiting game; somebody compared the government officials to "a bunch of vultures sitting in an old dead cottonwood tree, patiently waiting for its intended victim to die." But to everyone's surprise, the Indians hung on. Some journalists began calling the Indian occupation "the mouse that roared."

Yet the government was not about to give up; national honor was at stake. Another solution came up. If public support was the quartermaster of the Indian occupation, why not turn off the public?

"Conditions are ten times worse now," commented Don Carroll, former lighthouse keeper, in a sworn statement to James P. Southard, Special Agent of the GSA. Carroll went on to complain that the drains were clogged and raw sewage was being dumped into the basement of the old warden's house. He then added a little zinger. "Surely, Washington does not want to further public support for the Indian cause." Thomas Hannon supported Carroll's statements by adding that things had gone from bad to worse. He stated that responsible Indian leaders had left the island, and that Alcatraz had become nothing but an island ghetto.

I showed Cy Williams the newspaper reports of the Carroll and Hannon statements. He studied them for a while, then muttered, "First they took away the water barge so the toilets couldn't flush. Then they pulled the electrical power, turned up the heat with the fires, and now they are trying to bury us with bullshit."

Publicly, Hannon and Carroll criticized the harsh conditions on the island. But privately they must have gloated over the fact that the government had actually contributed to those virtually unlivable conditions. In some accounts, the media blamed the Indians for the deteriorated and rundown condition of the buildings, most of which were nothing more than empty shells. The buildings had been gutted of everything possible, and there was hardly anything left but rusted catwalks and barbed wire. Yet these conditions had been one of the reasons the government abandoned Alcatraz as a federal prison in 1963. A familiar story—the government criticizing conditions of Indian life which they themselves had created.

Government complaints about the condition of Alcatraz dragged on, as did the occupation. The enthusiasm, joy, and power of the early months were gone, and the action had the appearance of being mortally wounded. The government really didn't know what to do with the situation. They didn't want any arrests for trespassing, because that would take the case into court. They didn't want to use force, because that would cause problems with the media and the public. So they kept trying different angles. While one government group tried to negotiate through BANAC and cut services to make the Indians come to the bargaining table, another group tried to get the redskins off the island in a more secretive way.

The long history of government actions against native people has given Indians a built-in paranoia, and this paranoia was heightened during the occupation of Alcatraz. With so many people pouring into the Bay Area to participate and assist in the occupation in so many ways, it was impossible for the island residents to tell friend from foe. In the confusion, it was very easy for the government to infiltrate every aspect of Indian activity. Federal agencies not only observed and monitored the Indian activities on Alcatraz, but they also actively disrupted the occupation. They had to do something to offset the tremendous amount of public support the occupation received in its early months.During the 1960s the government tried many "dirty tricks" to undermine the various "radical" elements creating dissent in America. Many of these covert actions by the police and the FBI were later exposed, but damage had already been done. The Indian movement and the Alcatraz occupation were not spared.

In the book *Blood on the Land* Rex Weyler states:

> *FBI documents later obtained from the office of the Attorney General William Saxbe, through a Freedom of Information Act suit filed by NBC, revealed tactics*

used by the FBI to destroy the effectiveness of mili-
tant groups, including blacks, Communists and
Indians. The memoranda directed FBI offices to
"expose, disrupt, misdirect, discredit and otherwise
neutralize the groups, activities and individual names
of nationalist hate-type organizations and groupings,
their leadership, spokesmen, membership and
supports...prevent the rise of a 'Messiah' who can
unify and electrify the nationalist movement."

During his Watergate testimony, Presidential
counsel John Dean explained that "regular intelli-
gence reports" made from the FBI on "Indian upris-
ings" were sent to John Ehrlichman's aide Leonard
Garment, and that the Nixon administration "was
continually seeking intelligence information about
demonstration leaders and their supporters that
would either discredit them personally or indicate
that the demonstration was in fact sponsored by
some foreign enemy."

The FBI followed the Alcatraz occupation very closely. I guess they
were only doing their job, but I can't help but think it was a total waste
of time and money. They rented rooms in an expensive mainland motel
with a good view of Alcatraz. From there, they watched the island through
giant telescopes and long telephoto lenses on their cameras. It seems so
ludicrous that grown men spent eighteen months with their eyes glued to
big expensive telescopes, photographing even children in the hope of
catching them in some federal offense. But the more I think about it, the
more I can understand why the surveillance continued through the whole
occupation. If I was an FBI agent, I would rather sit in a plush hotel
peeking through a telescope than run around looking for some truly
dangerous criminals.

The "criminals" on Alcatraz had a boat that had been given to them
by a sympathetic rock band, Credence Clearwater Revival. The boat
gave the Indians the ability to independently shuttle people, food, and
supplies to Alcatraz, an independence which was very important to the
long term effort of holding the island. One morning the crew went down
to the dock and found the *Credence* sitting at the bottom of the murky
bay. How or why the boat sank will never be known for sure, as the
Indians did not have the money or equipment to raise the boat. But they
had a guess. Many of the Alcatraz Indians had served in the military;
some were fresh from fighting in Vietnam. They knew military tactics all

too well. It would have been easy for the government to send someone over to sink the boat.

The fires which burned much of Alcatraz, including the post exchange, warden's house, and adjoining lighthouse quarters were another mystery. Suspiciously, the fires started in two different places. Although the government claimed the fires were set by malcontent Indians upset with the stalemate in negotiations, the facts seemed to point the finger the other way. Just weeks before, the government had cut off all running water and electrical services to the island. Then two fires mysteriously broke out at the same time. Why then? It couldn't be coincidence. We will probably never know the answers with any certainty, but the government won a psychological victory in the battle for blame. Today, visitors tour the island and stare at the charred remains of the warden's house, once a beautiful example of Victorian architecture. Tour guides explain that the damage occurred during the Indian occupation, and the Indians are held accountable

The battle eventually came to what government officials termed the "last straw." The government had removed everything of value from the island when they abandoned it in 1962, but they left behind hundreds of yards of buried copper cable. Early in the occupation, three Indians "mined" the copper and sold it as salvage for $600. After eighteen months of FBI surveillance, this deed was all the FBI could come up with to justify removing the Indians from the island. Eighteen months of expenses to prosecute for only $600—only the government could justify that kind of budget.

Three men were accused of the year-old crime—Raymond Cox, 30; John D. Halloran, 27; and Frank J. Robbins, 32. They were brought to trial and found guilty by a jury. In spite of the conviction, Federal District Judge Ronald N. Davies could not hold back his personal feelings on the case. He chided the government for "vacillating" while the Indians held the island for a year and a half. He shook his head sadly as he looked at the federal prosecutor, James Bruen. "The U.S. officials handled the whole Alcatraz situation very badly in many areas," he said. "They vacillated, they couldn't make up their minds, and because of the conduct of certain government officials, there is a very great possibility these men may have thought they had the right to this copper." Judge Davies could have sentenced the three men to federal prison. Instead, he set a three-year probation.

Many Indians felt that the men should never have been brought to trial. One of the defendants remarked, "For 200 years the government has been stealing Indian lands and resources and we couldn't do a thing about it. Now, when we try to get some of it back, they make a federal case out of it!" He shrugged his shoulders in a helpless gesture. "I wonder how long it will take for us to receive justice in our own land?"

I had my own personal experience with the FBI; as an Indian leader I could only expect as much. One day during the occupation's prime, I received a phone call at my home in San Leandro. A man on the other end identified himself as part of a paramilitary group that made its headquarters in the Sierras. He uttered profanities about the government and its racist policies in the hopes of winning me over.

"We would like to offer our services to your warriors on Alcatraz. We have explosives and weapons and know how to use them," the voice said.

Warning bells went off in my head. We could always use support, but I didn't know if that was what he was really offering. Maybe his group was with the Weathermen, or maybe not. I tried to maintain my composure and politeness at the same time.

"Thank you for your offer, but we want to keep this an Indian protest and don't wish to have the occupation of Alcatraz tied to other issues." I hung up the phone, wondering what we might have started.

In the early 1980s, after I had been involved in the Indian cause for more than 20 years, I requested my federal records through the Freedom of Information Act. A package arrived that contained 57 pages about my role as an Indian activist, with five additional pages withheld for "security reasons." This came as a hell of a surprise to me, but the biggest shock came when I looked to see the who the enemy was and found that it was me!

One page was a report dated March 26, 1973, filed with the director of the United States Secret Service by L. Patrick Gray III, acting director of the FBI. He gave me a double mark in the category listing the reasons for surveillance: "potentially dangerous because of background, emotional instability, or activity in groups engaged in activities inimical to the U.S."

Some reports suggested that I had communist affiliations, and others stated that I was the Northern California President of the American Indian Movement (AIM). These allegations were all untrue, but being analyzed in this secretive manner was tantamount to being found guilty without benefit of a trial. The only real and truthful conclusion which the FBI had gathered about me was that I was "non-violent." I was shaken; if the FBI ever acted on its policy to "expose, disrupt, misdirect, discredit, and otherwise neutralize" I certainly had something to worry about.

On one very interesting page almost completely obliterated by censoring marks I found a very disturbing item—a record of the phone call to San Leandro. The FBI had deliberately baited me with the offer of violent activity. I guess I should be thankful that was as far as they went with me—other Indian leaders of later protests were not so lucky.

THE LAST DAY

No one had dared dream the occupation of Alcatraz would last for an incredible nineteen months, but it had. After so much time, life on Alcatraz had become very stagnant. The excitement had died down from the earlier months full of confrontation and active support, and public interest had turned elsewhere. With the Vietnam War still raging, anti-war protests growing steadily in number and size, the elections approaching, and other minorities protesting throughout the nation, the Indian occupation wasn't headline news anymore. The number of island inhabitants had dwindled to a token group, and the enthusiasm and sense of vision had also diminished. The island had become a gray, dull, and isolated place. The boredom, the unfulfilled dreams, and the lack of direction gave life on Alcatraz a certain resemblance to life on the reservations.

Yet on June 11, 1971, a beautiful day dawned on Alcatraz. It was the kind of late spring morning when people like to get things done and clean up after a long cold winter. A number of the occupants decided it was the perfect day to go to San Francisco. There were many chores to be done: shopping for groceries, filling up water containers, washing laundry, and enjoying a nice hot shower. Some went to visit friends and relatives on the mainland, perhaps to party it up since Alcatraz had lost its attraction as the hub of Indian activities. Content that all was going well, only fifteen Indians remained on the island. After all, it often seemed that Alcatraz belonged to the Indians—wasn't possession nine-tenths of the law? Mothers took care of their children, and others busied themselves with crafts. No lookouts were posted.

Warm weather had begun, and the maritime traffic around the bay had picked up as pleasure boats of all kinds took to the open waters. Sailboats, their multicolored sails resembling so many beautiful butter-flies, seemed to flit helterskelter around the bay. Their bright colors con-trasted sharply with the grey and rusting hulls of the ocean-going freighters struggling to reach the broad expanse of the Pacific Ocean against an incoming tide.

Tourists and visitors to the Bay Area always found this scene fasci-nating, but none of the Indians on Alcatraz paid attention to it anymore. If they had been more attentive, they would have spotted three Coast Guard cutters putting off from Yerba Buena Island, the island next to world-famous Treasure Island. Two of the cutters were 40 feet long, a size often seen around the bay, and the third was an 80-foot ocean-going cutter. Their gleaming white hulls displayed a blue chevron with the Coast Guard insignia. About 30 federal marshals and agents were on board; they all wore business suits and did not look at all like they were about to pull off a military landing. Their low-key appearance was part of the overall plan. The federal agents didn't want to draw attention to themselves, for if the news media got any idea of what was going down they would flock to the island to cover the scene. The marshals also wanted to avoid alerting the boat owners that were still friendly to the Indians and might support them.

What an interesting departure from history. In the old days we were attacked by cavalry soldiers on horseback. In modern times men wear-ing business suits and riding in motorized boats are the enemy, whether they are armed with guns or legal papers. Who can we really trust?

The three Coast Guard cutters made straight for the tiny dock facili-ties at Alcatraz, where the federal marshals started getting off. It wasn't the scenario one would expect of the U.S. Government taking over an island occupied by hostile Indians. The first Indian to spot the govern-ment men saw their business suits and assumed they were a bunch of news reporters. He thought nothing more of them until a friend shouted, "Damn, those guys got automatic weapons and shotguns!"

In a well-rehearsed raid, the marshals fanned out over the island, rounding up the women and children. Many of the Indians were terri-fied—they had never before looked down the barrel of a gun.

"Don't offer even token resistance, remember what happened at Wounded Knee!" shouted one of the Sioux men. Indians have long memories of the past, and the Alcatraz occupants were no exception. They didn't want to become the victims of an over-zealous federal mar-shal who might suddenly decide to spray them with high-velocity bullets from his automatic rifle.

Some of the women who wanted to go back into their apartments to gather up their meager belongings found the entrance blocked by a federal marshal with a rifle. "Look ladies, if you don't want to be put in handcuffs you'd better get back to the rest of the bunch!" he shouted.

The Indian men were also rounded up. The hunting knives some carried on their belts were confiscated, and everyone was searched for hidden weapons, although none were found. All together the federal marshals found only fifteen Indians on the island: six men, four women, and five children. The women and children were put in one group, the men in another, and they were all herded down to the dock and onto the Coast Guard cutters under "protective custody."

While the roundup was going on a Coast Guard helicopter circled the island searching for any Indians attempting to escape. The helicopter also kept away the curious onlookers in private boats who soon became aware of the unfolding drama. Word quickly spread to the news media, and some reporters paid $100 per person to charter boats out to the island. When they arrived, ten armed men in business suits who refused to identify themselves, or even admit they were government agents, threatened them with arrest. One local television station chartered a helicopter and actually landed on the island but beat a hasty retreat when armed federal marshals rushed toward the chopper with weapons at the ready.

The marshals combed the island for any Indians that might be hiding. With flashlights in one hand and automatic weapons in the other they searched every structure, including the ancient dungeons below the main cell block. When the marshals were satisfied that they had found everyone, the Coast Guard took the irate and disillusioned Indians to Yerba Buena Island, where they were searched again and interrogated. After giving the hungry Indians a late lunch the marshals told them that they would be taken back to San Francisco and dropped off. The Indians responded that they had no place to go in San Francisco; Alcatraz was their home. The marshals did not want to create another public outcry over poor treatment of the Indians, and so they took them to the Senator Hotel on Ellis Street in San Francisco.

While the Indians were being rounded up and removed, an additional force of federal marshals was landing on the island. The government called this unit a "protective force" which would be stationed on the island to provide security and keep unauthorized persons off the island. Their duties included installing a chain-link fence topped with barbed wire and patrolling the rocky shoreline with fierce guard dogs. Everything was part of a top-secret plan that had been worked out weeks before the actual removal.

The final decision to "recapture" Alcatraz was made by U.S. Attorney James L. Browning, Jr., along with Rear Admiral Mark Whalen, commander of the 12th Coast Guard District, and Thomas Hannon, regional director of the General Services Administration (GSA). The move made headline news throughout the Bay Area, and that evening I watched the press conference Browning called to explain the government action. I couldn't believe my ears when he stated that the theft of $600 in copper wire had been "the straw that broke the camel's back."

Browning went on to state, "The removal of illegal inhabitants had become an urgent necessity." Yet none of the Indians were arrested for trespassing, for obvious reasons. In a court of law the question of prior rights would certainly come up, and the government would be hard pressed to produce documents proving that they ever actually acquired the land from any of the local Indian tribes. The government avoided these questions by removing the Indians under threat and slamming the door behind them without any opportunity to test legality or morality in a court of law.

"We'll be back! We'll be back!" shouted Delbert Lee, a 22-year-old Sioux, and Atha White Man killer, a Cherokee, as they were taken from the island. Their promise had a hollow ring. Richard Oakes had made the same statement back on November 10, 1969, but things were different then, and we all knew it.

I turned off the television newscast so I could sit in the silence of my living room. The voice of Alcatraz leader John Trudell echoed in the quiet: "Browning lied to us! He promised there would be no actions against us while we were still negotiating." How very sad—for over 200 years, Indian leaders had been making similar statements and getting similar results.

The tragedy of the moment flooded over me, along with the realization that all our efforts of the last few years had come to a rather ignoble end. Yet the young warriors showed such passion as they shouted out, "We'll be back! We'll be back!" Their words demonstrated that the spirit of the Indian peoples had not been broken—we would persevere somehow. Sure, we made mistakes, a lot of them. After all, we were inexperienced in asserting our demands for justice in a country that gives lip service to the word but rarely practices it with the Indian people. But we were learning.

I also felt a sense of relief that it was all finished. Every important chapter in Indian history has ended with the removal of our people from the land, but life will and must go on. Our children need us.

THE REMOVAL

The Indians are being removed from Alcatraz Island by U.S. federal marshals.
June 11, 1971.

A second Coast Guard cutter with Indians and U.S. Marshals.

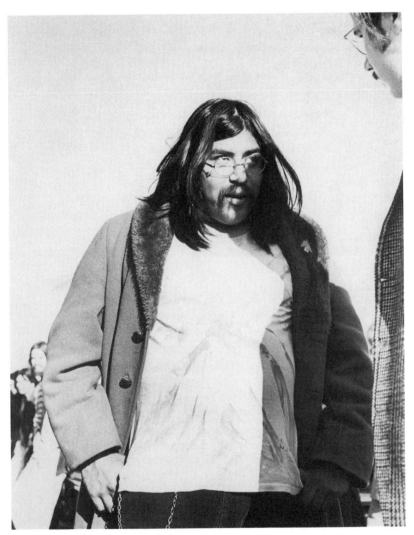

Occupier getting off the boat.

Above: Arriving at Pier 40.

Former occupiers of Alcatraz Island are back on the mainland.

Above: "We will not give up." Oohosis (Cree), left, and a friend.

Atha White Man Killer (Cherokee) at the Senator Hotel in San Francisco.

Atha White Man Killer at the press conference at the Senator Hotel.

Above: "We were using the island as a means of reminding the government that Indian people got rights."—John Trudell.

John Trudell at the press conference at the Senator Hotel.

Alcatraz children during the press conference.

June 11, 1971. The occupation is over.

THE SPIRIT LIVES ON

The government was determined that once the Indians were finally removed from the island they would never be able to return. Erwin N.
Thompson, who wrote a history of Alcatraz for the National Park Service, described the aftermath of the occupation:

> *The fire damage on the island was now supple-*
> *mented by the bulldozer's blade. To make the island*
> *inhospitable for any future army of occupation, the*
> *federal government had the apartment houses and*
> *other residences around the parade ground reduced*
> *to rubble. One of the machines was too large to get*
> *through the brick Sally Port of the historic*
> *guardhouse...one of the first structures erected on*
> *Alcatraz and well over 100 years old. The machine*
> *casually knocked out the brick arch, severely damag-*
> *ing the portal.*
>
> > *To make doubly sure that no reoccurrence of the*
> *occupation could take place, the GSA developed a*
> *plan and obtained an authorization for $50,000. The*
> *plan called for the installation of 2,500 feet of 8-foot*
> *chain link fence with three strands of barbed wire on*
> *top. There would be eighteen light standards for*
> *illumination, each bearing a cluster of three mercury*
> *vapor lights. The plan also called for fire guard posts*
> *manned by GSA guards and two sentry dogs.*

When Alcatraz was a federal prison it housed confirmed criminals, sex offenders, perpetrators of heinous offenses, and the most belligerent and physically aggressive gangsters, like "Scarface" Al Capone, "Machine Gun" Kelly, and members of the Barker-Karpis gang. Yet there were no extra security measures then—no chain link fence, no barbed wire, and no guard dogs. So it seems that the government was less concerned about keeping America's most feared and hardened criminals out of society than it was about keeping freedom-seeking Indians out of Alcatraz.

The effort to keep the Indians off Alcatraz did not stop with physically moving them, destroying their residences, or fencing off the island. The government also broke their promises that Indians would be involved in the new Alcatraz National Park. Lawrence Halperin, a well-known Bay Area architect, drew up plans to develop Alcatraz as a park. He held three meetings with over 100 concerned people, but he excluded Indians. The resultant plans for the island showed no signs of the promised "high Indian visibility."

The promises of the occupation all seemed to be history, so the United Council continued to pursue some of the original objectives for the island. We modified the proposals to accommodate the fact that Alcatraz had become a park, and then we set up a meeting with the new director of the Golden Gate National Recreation Association. The meeting did not go well. The director seemed to be cordial but wary, without any desire to pursue our plans.

BANAC also fell victim to broken promises. When the government realized that they no longer needed the group to help them resolve the issue of Alcatraz, the funding upon which BANAC depended was withdrawn. BANAC's collapse meant the end of the plans to create job training and employment assistance programs which would be more sensitive to Indian needs. The Indian centers, the United Council, Intertribal Friendship House, and most of the other organizations that had been in existence before Alcatraz continued their own programs. But for months and even years after Alcatraz ended, a sense of sadness, defeat, frustration, and betrayal hung heavily over the Indian community.

Yet even in our sadness we realized that we had gained an enormous victory. In the nineteen months of the occupation, Indians all over the country had gained far greater political power. The media had begun covering our concerns, and as a result non-Indians had learned of many of the injustices of the past centuries and the pain of current living conditions. Indians were filled with new-found pride. Alcatraz was a great awakening, one which even to this day changes our lives and stirs our souls.

After all, we realized our two immediate goals: we prevented commercial development of the island and we obtained a new Indian Center. In February of 1970, Dr. Dorothy Lone Wolf Miller personally carried $7,000 to the Bank of California for a down payment on a new Indian Center. The money came from our fund-raising campaign, which had prospered as a result of the Alcatraz occupation. The new center was a larger and better building than the one that had burned down in 1969, and it even included commercial rental space on the ground floor. No more worrying about landlords or rent increases—at long last, we had our own place.

I believe we also succeeded in terrifying the government. The prospect of an Indian uprising supported by a large liberal segment of the general population must have alarmed federal officials to no end. Guerrilla forces in Vietnam were humbling the mighty U.S. Army and paramilitary groups were forming throughout America. The government had good reason to be frightened of a strong Indian movement with a militant wing, especially when the Indians' complaints were so painfully real. So while the Alcatraz Indians were pressuring the government, federal officials were forced to negotiate with other Indian groups to appease the Indian community and stop further criticism from the general liberal population.

These new opportunities gave heart to many tribes throughout the country. Every study and every report published about Alcatraz added new credibility to the Indian viewpoint, and the occupation soon became the spark that lit fuses all over the country. More housing protests sprang up, and Indians "reclaimed" more than a dozen pieces of land for such places as Daybreak Star and D-Q U.

Daybreak Star began as Fort Lawton, a military installation near Seattle. At the time of the Alcatraz occupation the federal government was in the process of closing it down and selling it to the city of Seattle for the price of $1.00. The Indians in the Seattle area saw their chance, and decided direct action could have results.

On March 8, 1970, a group of Indians scaled the chain link fence surrounding the former military compound. Federal authorities removed them. Alcatraz veterans joined them for another attempt, and they were once again forcibly removed. The third attempt resulted in an occupation that lasted for three months and started negotiations between the Indians, the federal government, and the city of Seattle. The city and the new group of Indians of All Tribes consolidated their proposals in a friendly compromise: the Indians received twenty acres of Fort Lawton upon which to build a cultural center, which became known as "Daybreak Star." The community pitched in to help the project. A lumber company donated a truckload of huge logs for roof beams and support, and the City of Seattle Arts Program commissioned several Indian artists and sculptors to create pieces for the center. Daybreak Star became an established cultural center hosting many tribal and civic events and proudly adding to the cultural heritage of Seattle.

Another Indian success story is Deganawidah-Quetzalcoatl University, D-Q U, a joint Indian-Chicano University in Davis, California. As early as 1961, Jack Forbes (Powhattan) and Dave Risling (Hupa) envisioned an Indian University for the state of California. Over the years they developed ideas and prepared proposals. They found an abandoned military communications center near Davis and filed the proper application to secure the unused land as a university site. Once again, the bureaucratic run-around began. In October of 1970, U.S. Senator Murphy issued a press release stating that the site would be awarded instead to the University of California.

The Indians and Chicanos were furious with Senator Murphy's decision and decided to try the tactics of Alcatraz . On November 3, 1970, they climbed the fence around the site and took possession of the land. The next day, warriors and women of Alcatraz joined them.

Finding themselves in an unexpected dilemma, the University of California withdrew its proposal for the land. The federal government realized that the protestors had called their bluff and gave in to their demands. On April 2, 1971, "Deed Day," the first Native American college in America finally opened its doors, and a large and happy crowd of Indian and Chicano supporters attended the opening ceremony. As Chairman of the United Council, I presented a peace pipe "to acknowledge our spiritual heritage to the land" and several ears of Indian corn "symbolizing the seeds of knowledge being planted on this land." After the ceremony, a federal official approached Jack Forbes and inquired, "Now can you get those damn Indians off Alcatraz?"

There were other attempts to take surplus land, although they were not always so successful . One incident occurred in the city of New York, which had a large Indian population and an active Indian center, the Indian Community House, similar to the ones in Oakland and San Francisco. Glowing media accounts of the Alcatraz occupation awakened ideas in the New York Indian community, and visits by Alcatraz veterans John Trudell and Rain Parrish stirred the ideas to action. Ellis Island had been used in earlier years to process European immigrants. It had come to symbolize freedom for many Americans, and it now stood vacant. It was too tempting to pass up.

The New York Indians attempted to invade, but due to poor planning, reluctance to use white support, and a leaky boat, the attempt

Children at D-Q U opening ceremony. Photograph courtesy of Ilka Hartmann.

failed completely. The Coast Guard and the FBI stepped in and threatened anyone who invaded the island again with dire consequences. Recognizing the futility of any further attempts, the Indians abandoned the liberation of Ellis Island. Yet the government realized that if they didn't do something to appease the Indians, any unoccupied land anywhere in the country was going to be up for grabs.

Opposition continued to spread. Housing protests began in Chicago, Indians protested for fishing rights in the state of Washington and northern California, and other protests sprang up across the nation. But even more significant was the change in government policy that brought an end to the misguided programs of relocation and termination. Within weeks of the invasion the Department of the Interior quietly and abruptly ended the program of relocation, an action that had seemed likely to languish for years in the courts.

Changes continued. On July 8, 1970, eight months into the Alcatraz occupation, President Richard Nixon signed the Indian Self-Determination Act into law. He sent a message to Congress declaring the policy of termination to be "morally and legally unacceptable." For decades since the Termination Act, the U.S. Government had been terminating the status of Indian tribes as independent nations with their own lands. Tribal lands were turned into private property, and tribes lost many of their services. Chaos ensued, and generations of Native Americans lost their heritage and culture.

Nixon urged Congress to "remove, repudiate, and repeal" this policy. By executive order of the President, astonishing amounts of land were returned to their native peoples. 45,000 acres of the Sacred Blue Lakes reverted to the Taos Pueblo people, and more than 160,000 acres, with access to the Columbia River, reverted to the Warm Springs tribes of Oregon. Many land claims still remained unsettled, and the fight continued over places like the Black Hills or Wounded Knee, where another period of bloodshed eventually took place. Still, it seemed that the government, at least for the moment, heard a new and truthful message from the Indian people and cautiously rethought its course to their destruction.

Are we justified in attributing such benefits to Alcatraz, or is this credit just a fantasy of those who fought so hard for the island? I recently asked Robert Bennett, former Commissioner of Indian Affairs, to consider what might have happened to the Indian people if we had not occupied Alcatraz. He responded, "There was a real danger that all would have been lost." He then added, "It also helped awaken Indian tribes from their complacency."

Bennett later remarked, "One of the first and direct results of Alcatraz was that the BIA started working with state employment agencies on a cooperative basis to find jobs for Indians on or near the reservations." This policy replaced the former programs of relocation. He also described a change in the attitude of the BIA. "We started to listen more to young Indian leadership. The old guard, the old tribal leaders, were the ones we had listened to for many years. Instead, we began listening to the new voices of the young."

As the oppressive cloud of termination lifted and the new policies began, Indian tribes once again planned for their future. Another social experiment with the American Indian was officially over; another chapter of the historic relationship between the federal government and the tribes had come to an ignoble ending.

Yet the most lasting result of Alcatraz may have been the growth of Indian pride throughout the country. News of the occupation swept through Indian communities; our continued resistance inspired wonder and pride. After decades of indignity and soul-sickening powerlessness beyond the understanding of any non-Indian, a group of Indians had seized an island in full view of millions and held it for nineteen months despite government efforts to destroy them. Everywhere, American Indians rejoiced.

One of our original goals for Alcatraz had been to set up an institute of higher learning, an Indian college. I think that in ways we were successful beyond our wildest dreams. We educated an entire country about Indian life, and the experience of the occupation educated many Indians who went on to become leaders and spokespeople in the Indian movement. The spirit and the lessons of Alcatraz became part of history and can never be lost.

We lost the island itself, but Indian loss of land is nothing new in this country. I mourn our loss—the loss of the land, the loss of the dream. But I also rejoice, and I am fiercely proud of what we won. At the beginning of Alcatraz, I started to let my hair grow long in the traditional way. All Indian men wore their hair long until the whites came to our land and killed our ways, even cutting off our hair. In memory of Alcatraz, and as a symbol of my dedication to Indian causes, I have not cut my hair since. And as long as I live, I never will.

PAST AND FUTURE

Years went by, and eventually we approached the fifth anniversary of the occupation of Alcatraz. The United Council made plans for a special ceremony to commemorate the event. The Intertribal Dancers and the Mockingbird Singers began rehearsing a special ceremonial dance, to be performed on a return visit to the island. We wanted everything to be right and proper for the day, and many of us helped round up traditional dance accessories.

Bobbie and I were feeling special cause for celebration. Our daughter Julie and her husband Steve Titus were expecting their first child, and they had asked that we name the baby. This was a great honor, for they did not want just any name, but an Indian name. Ever since their Indian wedding at D-Q U earlier in the year, when they had made the request, Bobbie and I had been pondering a variety of names.

In our traditions, there are several ways of giving a name. A name has spirit power and should be appropriate to the child whenever possible. It can be a hereditary name, a clan name, a dream name, an earned name, or a name that comes from something important or unusual which happens on the day of the birth.

As the baby would be our first grandchild, we were both a little anxious, especially since we knew that the birth was rapidly approaching and time was running out for finding a name. As we made our way out to the island that November day in 1974, we marveled at the ease and comfort we enjoyed on the spacious deck of the tour boat, compared to the cramped decks of fishing boats or private crafts we had used during the occupation. As we approached the island, happy shouts went up from the Indians crowding the rail.

"Alcatraz! Alcatraz! We have come back, our friend!"

We peered across the waters looking for familiar landmarks and delighting in the prospect of a great reunion between the earth people and the stone person of Alcatraz. Once on shore we began to make our way up the narrow winding road to the pinnacle of the island. As we crossed the familiar moat below the ancient and decrepit drawbridge, I paused to look up at the keystone of the archway. Once again, I read the faint Spanish inscription: "Isla de Alcatraces," or "Island of the Pelicans." To the Indian, the phrase meant "Island of the Water Birds."

Once again, I had a spiritual conversation with the drawbridge. A physical silence overcame me, allowing other forms of communication to take place.

"Drawbridge, Drawbridge, we have once again returned," the silent, mystical dialogue began.

"Welcome back, my friends," responded the Drawbridge. "What request do you make of me this time?"

"No request this time," I answer, "for this time we have returned with prayers and thanksgiving to you. You gave our people sanctuary and hope, and now we have come to acknowledge you, to honor you, to say mi-gwitch and give thanks. It is also our hope that we may do so year after year."

"I am pleased and honored that you are doing this, but are you sure that you have no request to make of me?" questioned Drawbridge.

"Well, yes. Maybe just a small request. We have a new child being born and we are in need of a name," I said hopefully.

"Why don't you name the child after me. It would be nice to have a Weh-eh, a namesake," suggested Drawbridge, chuckling lightly now.

"You want to name the child Drawbridge?" I asked in disbelief.

"No, no! I mean name the child after what this island represents— water birds!" said Drawbridge, laughing over the misunderstanding.

"Thank you! Thank you!" I shouted as I ran up the road to catch up with the group. How appropriate, how nice. As I reached Bobbie's side, I gave her the good news, and she immediately agreed to the symbolism. An appropriate Indian name would now be bestowed.

We made our way to the main yard of the prison, the site of our first Thanksgiving on the island five years earlier. Standing in a large circle, everyone was blessed and smudged with fragrant sweet-grass smoke in a spiritual cleansing and purification. In this way it was certain that everyone was with good heart, good mind, and good body. Hostility and anger would not come to the scared circle we had created.

With pure hearts and mind we held the sacred pipe in a modified "Wash-Away-the-Tears" ceremony, and our prayers were sent to the Great Spirit. We asked for safe care for our ancestors and some of the new arrivals to the Spirit World: Yvonne Oakes, who died of injuries in a fall on the island; Richard Oakes, leader of the early days of the occupation; and Ethel Raigoma, who died in a car accident while delivering food and supplies to Alcatraz. We gave prayers of appreciation for what Alcatraz had achieved. We drank water, symbolizing the washing away of tears and at the same time acknowledging that water is the blood of our Earth Mother. Our drinking signified the renewal and continuation of life itself.

Everyone then became very happy, for life is for the living to share and enjoy. We are never to forget those loved ones who precede us to the Spirit World, but there is a time to set aside the grieving. We busied ourselves with preparations for the next part of the ceremony. Leonard Harrison put on his splendid tribal outfit, and we handed him a shield and spear. The women prepared themselves, but in a very different manner than was traditional. They donned the eagle-feather war bonnets of the men and carried shields and spears. The spectators standing at the far end of the area had no idea what we were doing.

Chuck Snow, a Shoshone from Wyoming, was the lead singer for the ceremony. He had taught the other Mockingbird Singers a special song which had only been performed once before in the Bay Area. We didn't know it at the time, but the second performance would also be the last.

Usually, the singers sit around a large bass drum to sing the pow wow songs. This time, each singer held his own hand drum, and they all formed a line on the west side of the yard. The seven male singers faced the female dancers, and Chuck Snow began the song.

Not only was the song different, but the beat on the drums was also different. It was hauntingly beautiful. Without urging, the Indian spectators stood up out of respect for the ceremonial dance about to be performed.

The women in their war bonnets had also formed a line. They danced in place to the throbbing, hypnotic beat of the drums. Leonard started dancing back and forth along the line of singers, then turned and approached the line of women. Holding up his shield and spear, he advanced toward their line, whooping in challenge as he approached.

The women held their line until Leonard was almost upon them, then they let out war whoops of their own and all danced forward in a line, waving their spears back and forth. Leonard retreated before them, back toward the line of singers. The women then returned to their original line. Leonard started his advance again, only to retreat once again as the woman advanced toward him. They danced this back-and-forth dance four times.

Leonard represented the threat to the village, and the women dressed in the headdresses of warriors represented the defenders of the village. Leonard's fourth retreat back to the line of singers represented the end of his aggression. When the threat had left, the women formed a circle, rejoicing as they danced the victory celebration of the Shoshone. The pageantry and powerful symbolism of the dance also represented Alcatraz, for it has seen four different forms in its history—the fort, the prison, the Indian land, and last the national park.

The staff of many feathers, set in the ground at the celebration, carried the four sacred colors of red, white, yellow, and black, which symbolize the four colors of man. The final circle dance of the ceremony represented the joining of the sacred hoop—the people of the four sacred colors coming together as Brothers and Sisters. They join in the hope that all life forms that share the Earth Mother may live in balance and harmony. It may be just an idealistic hope and dream, but if we don't work for the goal, it will never happen.

And on that special day a child was born. Benayshe-ba-equay, Bird-of-the-Water-Woman. A new and special life, a new hope for the future.

ADAM FORTUNATE EAGLE

Adam Fortunate Eagle was born as Adam Nordwall in 1929 on the Chippewa reservation in Red Lake, Minnesota. As was customary federal policy at that time, he was taken from his parents in childhood and sent to Indian boarding schools where it was forbidden to practice tribal customs or speak tribal languages. He met his wife, Bobbie, while both were attending Haskell Indian Institute in Kansas.

Following graduation from Haskell, the couple married and moved to San Francisco, California, where Adam began work for an extermination firm. He later formed his own business in Oakland, California, where in the 1950s he met Indians from all over the country who had been forced into the area under the federal program of relocation.

It was through these social contacts that Adam first became involved in the urban intertribal pow wow gatherings. He eventually began participating in the political organizations of the urban Indian community. From 1962–1976, he served as Chairman of the United Council. In 1973 Adam "discovered" Italy in a widely-publicized turnabout of the claims of Columbus.

Adam was given the name "Fortunate Eagle" when he was adopted into the Whistling Water Clan of the Crow Nation. He and Bobbie currently live on her Shoshone-Paiute reservation near Fallon, Nevada, where Adam operates an art gallery. He is recognized as a pipe carrier, or ceremonial leader, among tribal elders and continues to travel extensively in the United States and Europe as a visiting artist and lecturer on Native American customs and rights.

VINE DELORIA, JR.

Vine Deloria, Jr. (Standing Rock Sioux) is a professor at the University of Colorado at Boulder, and the author of *Custer Died for Your Sins*.

ILKA HARTMANN

Ilka Hartmann came to California from Germany in 1964. Soon afterwards, she met her first American Indian at a California mission. While attending UC Berkeley, she demonstrated to support the Native American Studies Program. One foggy morning, she read that during the night Indians had rowed to Alcatraz and seized the island. She visited Alcatraz as soon as she could, and returned again and again. By great luck, she was there when the Indians were taken off the island. Her pictures of the occupation were published in underground papers and shown in the Indian community.

Ilka began to attend Indian events all over the Bay Area, hitchhiking and sleeping on people's floors. She met Adam Fortunate Eagle two or three times during these days, although he doesn't remember her. Ever since, Ilka has been documenting contemporary American Indian life in the cities and on the reservations. Her photographs have been published and exhibited in the United States and in Germany.